10 Natural Forces *for* Business Success

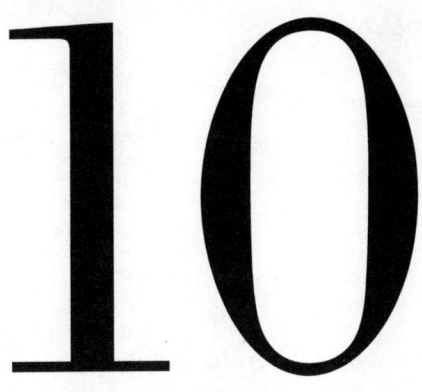

10

Natural Forces *for*

Business Success

HARNESSING THE ENERGY
FOR POSITIVE IMPACT

Peter R. Garber

DAVIES-BLACK PUBLISHING, INC.
Palo Alto, CA

Published by Davies-Black Publishing, a division of CPP, Inc., 3803 East Bayshore Road, Palo Alto, CA 94303; 800-624-1765.

Special discounts on bulk quantities of Davies-Black books are available to corporations, professional associations, and other organizations. For details, contact the Director of Book Marketing and Sales at Davies-Black Publishing, 3803 East Bayshore Road, Palo Alto, CA 94303; 650-691-9123; fax 650-623-9271.

References to *Future Edge* (1992) and *Wealth, Innovation, & Diversity* (2001) used by permission of Joel A. Barker. Barker's films can be purchased by calling 1-800-PARADIGM.

06 05 04 03 02   10 9 8 7 6 5 4 3 2 1
Printed in the United States of America

Library of Congress Cataloging-in-Publication Data
Garber, Peter, R.
10 natural forces for business success: harnessing the energy for positive impact / Peter R. Garber.
p. cm.
Includes bibliographical references and index.
ISBN 0-89106-169-X
1. Success in business. I. Title: Ten natural forces for business success. II. Title.

HF5386 .G2128 2002
650.1—dc21   2002023414

FIRST EDITION
First printing 2002

Contents

My Forces

Over the years, a number of forces have significantly influenced my life, and they have contributed greatly to this book. Naturally, these include the most important people in my life. First and foremost are my beautiful wife, Nancy, and my terrific teenage daughters, Lauren and Erin. They are truly the driving forces in my life.

Other important forces have been less direct but still very influential. My career as a human resources professional with PPG Industries, Inc., has provided a wealth of learning opportunities and discoveries over the more than 20 years of our association. The time I spent as a corporate training and development specialist helped initiate my understanding of many of the ten Natural Forces. Although I did not completely understand their full influence at the time, I now realize that almost every training program I presented focused on one or more of these Natural Forces.

A number of authors have been major factors in the development of this book. Dr. Stephen Covey and his wonderful book *The 7 Habits of Highly Effective People* have together had a great impact on my life, both personally and professionally. Another very significant force has been futurist Joel Barker and his theories about paradigms. Others include Ken Blanchard, Philip Crosby, Tom Peters, and Peter Senge, to name just a few. Each has in his own way contributed to my understanding of one or more of the Natural Forces.

There is one other person who has been very significant in helping me develop the concepts presented in this book. His name is Harold Shafer, but he prefers to be called Shaf. My self-appointed mentor during most of my career, he also has become one of my closest friends. When I started my career with PPG, Shaf was the head of the company's Glass Business's Training Group. As a young human resources trainee, I marveled at his ability to explain complex concepts in a clear and understandable manner. He shared his optimistic view of the world, explaining that exceptions to acceptable job performance were the fault of the system rather than of individuals. He taught us that it was our job as managers to fix the system and not blame others for problems or point fingers. As part of his training programs, Shaf took us places by supporting the concepts he taught with mental images so real that we might have sworn we were there. Looking back on those lessons from my old friend, I now realize that much of what he taught us was really about the Natural Forces. I had the privilege of becoming Shaf's understudy during his last year of work before he retired to the Outer Banks of North Carolina. Shaf generously shared with me much of his unique wealth of knowledge about organizations and people, which he had acquired during his distinguished 30-year career. There are a great many of these lessons from Shaf in the chapters that follow.

Thanks once again, Shaf, and everyone else who has contributed to this book. You have all been very positive forces in my life.

About the Author

Peter R. Garber is Manager of Affirmative Action for PPG Industries, Inc., in Pittsburgh, Pennsylvania. He has been with PPG since 1980 and has held a variety of human resources positions. He was Manager of Teamwork Development for PPG prior to taking on his current assignment of providing consultative services, training, seminars, and guidance on a wide variety of management topics to associates at all levels of the organization.

Garber is the author of six business-related books, including *Turbulent Change: Every Working Person's Survival Guide, Coaching Self-Directed Work Teams,* and *Managing by Remote Control,* and is coauthor of the popular *101 Stupid Things Supervisors Do to Sabotage Success.* He has also published a number of articles and teaching tools on a variety of human resources and business subjects.

Garber received his bachelor's degree in English from the University of Pittsburgh and his master's degree in guidance and personnel from St. Bonaventure University. He is married and has two daughters. He and his family reside in Pittsburgh.

Introduction

M any of the organizational problems we confront on a daily basis can be better understood and resolved if we just pay more attention to what's natural. Gaining a better understanding of the ten Natural Forces in organizations presented in this book will help you begin this learning journey. The ten Natural Forces are *Survival, Change, Communication, Mission, Equity, Performance, Discovery, Diversity, Growth,* and *Renewal.* These forces are often the reason for organizational success or failure even though they seldom get the blame or credit for the way things turn out. Your approach to dealing with these forces may have a great deal to do with your success as a manager or leader in your organization.

Think of these forces as a flock of geese flying in formation. Geese flying in this manner travel about 70 percent faster than do those that fly alone. They support one another in their flight. When

the leader tires, another takes its place. They communicate constantly, honking from behind to encourage those in front. If a goose is injured or ill, others stop and provide assistance.

The flock of geese shown above and repeated at the beginning of chapters 1 through 10 will serve as a reminder that the ten Natural Forces work in harmony with one another. Although each is very influential by itself, they are extraordinarily powerful as a combined force. Looking at them together will help you understand how each one is affected by the others. You need to consider their collective impact on the organization as well as their individual influences.

If Natural Forces are not adequately addressed, serious problems will arise. Left unattended, these forces may go awry or spin out of control. When interventions cease or countermeasures run their course, Natural Forces will return and take over again. As Natural Forces gain momentum, they may be even harder to control.

One of the most difficult aspects of these forces is that they exist whether or not management approves of or even understands them. Even though you may not realize it, much of your organization's current policies and practices are probably based on dealing with Natural Forces. Misunderstanding Natural Forces causes misinterpretation of problems and can create false relationships in the minds of managers. These associations become almost like superstitions. It's like carrying a rabbit's foot around in your briefcase—there seems to be a connection between behaviors or actions and results, but no one understands what it is. You do certain things, thinking that your actions will lead to certain results, when in reality the outcomes are more likely a function of unnoticed Natural Forces. Lack of understanding of Natural Forces is one of the most serious and common management mistakes. If you don't understand the Natural Forces and their influence on your organization, you may continue to deal with the same problems over and over again because you never really get to the root of the issues at hand.

To optimize the chances of success, organizations should build both their operational and their personnel systems around Natural Forces, which have enormous innate energy. Helping the organization tap into this energy may be one of the most important contributions you can make in your career as a manager or leader. Harnessing this energy can be one of the most effective and cost-saving initiatives that your organization may ever undertake. Understanding Natural Forces will enable you to better utilize their power and energy to reach your personal and professional goals for success.

Like the weather, organizational Natural Forces are often very unpredictable. Unfortunately, you cannot simply tune into the latest forecast to find out about the next Natural Force that may be heading for your organization. You must rely on your own ability and even your intuitions concerning the inevitable arrival of these Natural Forces in your organization. This book will help you become a better forecaster of Natural Forces. It will explain how you can learn not only to identify and understand them but how to make them work for you.

Survival

Equity   Mission   Communication   Change   Survival   Performance   Discovery   Diversity   Growth   Renewal

LAWS OF THE SURVIVAL NATURAL FORCE

- Survival is the most basic need.

- Survival has many faces.

- The Survival Natural Force can be unpredictable.

- Survival has emotional costs.

Charles Darwin's theories of evolution and natural selection came as a shock to much of the world in 1859. But in the early 21st century, it certainly should surprise no one that an organization's survival is based on its ability to adapt to the ever-changing business environment.

Survival Is the Most Basic Need

Survival is an innate drive in all human beings, and organizations as a whole are no different. The need to survive is the most basic of all the Natural Forces.

For employees, survival in an organization means steady employment; for the organization, it means maintaining operations. Once a basic level of survival is assured (at least for the moment), the next level requires feeling secure that the situation will continue (at least for the immediate future). In employees' eyes, it means being able to depend on the organization to provide jobs and paychecks as long as they choose to work for the company. For the organization, it means being able not only to sustain current levels of profitability but to improve performance (see chapter 6).

Employees are usually much more perceptive about issues of security than they are given credit for, especially when it comes to sensing threats to their personal survival. Workforces have been raised on the "feast or famine" cycles of the business economy. They know how quickly fortunes can disappear and fates can change. They know when their leadership is struggling desperately to deal with declining performance and dismal financial results. Management almost always underestimates employees' information sources and networking capacities, which enable them to monitor what is really going on in the organization (discussed further in chapter 3). Managers don't take into account that employees read newspapers and magazines, watch television, and are very astute at sensing signs that their survival might be in jeopardy. Employees know when business is bad. They are the ones who perform such tasks as loading the trucks, shipping the goods, and answering the phones, and they are fully aware when business is slipping. They recognize the reverse situation as well. They know when business is improving and will want their fair share of the success they helped achieve (see chapter 5).

They have a keen sense of the Natural Force of Survival. It is this drive to survive that perpetuates a species. Without it, there would be no struggle to overcome the tremendous challenges of existence.

Chrysler's battle to survive during the early 1980s provides a good example of the power of the Survival Natural Force. At that time, higher-quality, lower-cost Japanese imports were taking over the American automotive marketplace, and Chrysler was on the verge of going out of business. Led by the now legendary CEO Lee Iacocca, the company fought for its survival by engaging the entire nation in its struggle. It utilized a media campaign and political lobbying and garnered an unprecedented $1.2 billion government loan to keep itself afloat.

This American success story illustrates the will to survive despite overwhelming odds. Chrysler, with Iacocca at the helm, went on to introduce what was at the time a revolutionary vehicle—the minivan. It became one of the best-selling vehicles in North America and is the gold standard of minivans to this day. The drive to survive brought Chrysler from the brink of extinction to a position of prominence in the competitive automotive business through the support of the buying public and the U.S. government.

Survival Has Many Faces

In organizations, survival may take many forms, not all of which are easily recognized or productive. In the quest for survival, people may take measures and resort to actions that are counterproductive. For example, employees may leave the company in search of security, but then, as the most recently hired at their new places of employment, they find themselves in a less secure situation. The Natural Force of Survival will be used to justify many other behaviors that might not otherwise be acceptable. Massive downsizing, employee turnover, contract cancellations, and policy violations, to name a few, are all based on the Survival Force in organizations. Faced with a threat to survival, typically benevolent and nurturing organizations turn into cold, cruel career executioners, sending many of their most loyal and hardworking employees out onto the street. To make matters worse, they do this during times when jobs are most difficult to find and economic conditions are most precarious.

The Survival Natural Force Can Be Unpredictable

One need only look at the meteoric rise and abrupt fall of the dot-com industry in the first year of this new century to appreciate the volatility of today's business environment. One of the factors behind the sudden reversal of fortunes was the revolutionary growth of this high-tech industry, fueled by the introduction and popularity of the Internet. These developments were the electronic age's equivalent of a major cultural climate change, which affected the very survival of more traditional industries. Instead of growing at a conventional pace, the dot-com industry exploded onto the scene almost overnight.

Before the industry crash, high-tech employees couldn't be brought in fast enough, but they were being laid off literally by the thousands just a few months later. Even technology leaders that had been the darlings of the NASDAQ less than a year earlier—AOL, Intel, Lucent—announced massive layoffs in 2001. These events dramatically changed the sense of security felt by the organizations, their employees, and investors. In many ways, the dot-com industry's sudden crash can be likened to a natural disaster that threatens the existence of an evolving species.

There is perhaps no more telling cultural evidence of this industry's overnight success and even faster demise than the record number of commercial minutes purchased for Super Bowl XXXIV on January 30, 2000. The majority of this extraordinarily expensive ($2.3 million for a 30-second spot) advertising time was bought by a number of young Internet companies, most of which no longer existed a year later when the dot-com industry's growth came to an end; a mere 3 of the 20 advertisers remained. The lesson here is that phenomenal success such as that enjoyed by the dot-com industry in 1999 and early 2000 doesn't guarantee survival even a relatively short time later.

Survival Has Emotional Costs

Security is an emotional state. It is constantly being sought but is also very fragile. A workforce's collective sense of security needs continuous nourishment. Times of change, even if they do not involve a challenge to survival, also create demands on management to address the turmoil and stress that people naturally experience in these situations.

Because survival is such a basic Natural Force, it is important to address the issue frequently with employees, even when change is not currently taking place. People need constant reminders of the power of this Natural Force and assurances that, at least for the moment, their survival is not being threatened. You can hardly do this too often, particularly as things begin to change. However, take care not to create a false sense of security, or you may destroy the organization's future credibility among employees. Conversely, the survival card shouldn't be played too often or without justification. This tactic will quickly be perceived as "crying wolf," and when real danger emerges, no one will pay attention. It doesn't take too many false warnings to lose the trust and attention of your workforce, which take years to build and only milliseconds to lose. Be careful with people's emotions, particularly when their survival is involved. Survival is not something to play games with or take lightly.

It is also important to remember how quickly people forget what it was like to be endangered. Perhaps they don't want to remember or think about the intensely difficult and stressful conditions this Natural Force creates. Commitments or deals that might have been struck during times of survival, even if only psychological, may no longer be considered valid. It's like the person who goes to his lawyer and says, "I'll give you anything if you can only get me out of this problem I got myself into!" Of course, this individual feels quite different once the heat is off and he gets his attorney's bill. The point is that we can't constantly live on the edge emotionally. There are special times in our lives that present both challenges and opportunities, and survival often brings out the best and the worst in us. Managers must realize that a continuum of emotions exists when this Natural Force is emerging, present, or ending.

Survival Stages

Survival is a process that occurs in stages, with each stage enabling the next. Gaining a better understanding of these stages will improve your ability to adapt to the changes you inevitably must face.

Security

The first stage of survival is *security*. We typically have no real consciousness of being in a secure state. Like oxygen, security makes us keenly aware of its existence by its absence. If the oxygen level were to drop suddenly and dramatically, you soon would be unable to focus on anything else in your immediate environment. You may not consider a particular time in your life secure until you see what lies ahead that makes the past seem like the "good old days."

Change Event

The next stage of the survival process is the introduction of a *change event*. A change event is an occurrence that transforms the status quo. It ends what is currently going on in the workplace. A change event can be an extremely stressful experience for everyone. It takes people out of their comfort zones and into territory that seems strange and different. People yearn for the so-called good old days, when they felt safe and comfortable. They might begin to feel insecure about the implications and possible consequences of the change event. Will it alter their lives in such a way that things can never be put back in their original places? This is perhaps the most difficult part of the survival process at work. People don't mind change as much as they mind being changed themselves. Losing a sense of security and being thrust into the unknown can be very traumatic and may cause displays of maladaptive behaviors. The consequences of and management approaches to these types of behaviors will be discussed in more detail later in this chapter.

Searching

At first, *searching* behaviors are usually focused on returning to where you have been. In many ways, it is similar to denial. You don't want to accept what has happened or the changes being thrust upon you. The good old days seem even better now that they are behind you.

During periods of organizational change, people at first search for answers as to whether a change event is about to occur and then want to know why it happened. Understanding the reasons behind change and the meaning of the change itself helps people reach closure. The worst thing that can happen is to attach no meaning to the change event. People need to believe that there is a reason for everything they are going through in dealing with change.

Adaptation

Gaining understanding in the searching stage leads people to *adaptation,* when they adjust to their new circumstances and situations.

They can then say to themselves, "I am going through all of this anxiety and trauma _____." The blank could be filled with any number of reasons. Ideally, they might fill in the blank with statements that sound like ". . . because we need to restructure the organization to meet competitive pressures or we won't survive as a company." However, they could also complete the sentence with something that sounds more like ". . . and I don't have the slightest clue as to why this is happening to me." Obviously, there is a big difference between these two mind-sets. The discrepancy demonstrates just what an important role the Natural Force of Change, discussed next, plays in this process.

Adaptation is the first really positive step in the survival process. It signals the transformation from clinging desperately to the past to accepting the future. Adaptation requires people to change. Again, this is often the toughest part. As Darwin discovered, if a species doesn't adapt, it won't survive change. Employees in an organization that is experiencing change are no different. Only those who adapt to the change event will survive. However, it is fair to mention at this point that survival can mean many things in an organization. The basic, or lowest, level of survival is to still have a job, but this level can lead to what might be called *Dead Careers Walking*. These people still appear on the reporting chart, but their careers are suffering from a terminal illness called *job apathy*.

People have the inherent ability to adapt to nearly any situation, but they need the resources to be able to make this transformation. A single missing resource can keep a person from adapting to his or her new environment. With it, a person can do amazingly creative things; without it, there may no option but to give up on trying to adapt. One of the most important keys to being an effective manager is to understand what these critical resources might be and ensure that they are provided to employees. The challenge, of course, is to sift through all the many other demands for resources and identify which ones are critical and which are not.

Resolution

Believe it or not, there is at least one *resolution* to every problem. The difficulty is that this resolution may not be the one everyone wants. One resolution for the plummeting dot-com industry in the beginning of 2001 presumably was to implement massive employee layoffs. The carnage helped reduce costs in response to the dramatic drop in capital being poured into these companies compared to just a short year before.

Resolutions may also involve risk. A decision to resolve a problem might be either the best thing that ever happened to the organization or the worst. High-tech companies like Lucent that reduced their workforce by the thousands in the wake of the dot-com crash may have done the only thing possible to ensure their survival during the rapid downturn the industry was experiencing. Or, instead, they may have weakened themselves by losing many of their experienced workers and may be unable to recover fully when the high-tech slump is over. The ultimate judge of such decisions is time. It takes courage to take these risks, and not everyone is willing to throw the dice on this kind of gamble. As we will see in the final stage, survival doesn't always bring with it everything that everyone hopes for or expects.

Reality

The last phase of the survival process can often be the most difficult, for it requires facing *reality*. Our hopes and dreams for the future may contain unrealistic visions of what things will be like when and if we get to the next phase in our lives. We sometimes think in terms of "If only X would happen, my life would be so much better." This kind of thinking only sets us up for big letdowns.

Managers must be aware of this tendency and not contribute to unrealistic thinking through promises or innuendo. It is all too easy to try to bolster morale during difficult economic times with images of a promised land that awaits those who are able to weather the storm. This approach will only cause morale and attitudes to be even worse after the immediate crisis is over, when people begin to realize that their expectations are not going to be met. As a result, this Natural Force will spin out of your control. A realistic vision of survival must be conveyed (see chapter 4). Dealing with the realities of survival is much easier if people have a realistic picture of what to expect and hope for in the future.

Managing the Survival Natural Force

Without a crystal ball in which to see the future, you will never know the ultimate outcome of your decisions. On the one hand, you don't want to be paralyzed into inaction by the fear of failure. This could cause you to ignore great opportunities that, once past, will never be duplicated. On the other hand, you don't want to risk the corporation's assets on investments that turn into a money drain and fail to meet any of the organization's intended objectives. This "bet the family farm" investment mentality has been responsible for the decline and demise of too many companies. One has only to look at how may "farms" were bet on the dot-com industry in 2000 to understand what is at risk.

Decision Making and the Survival Force

Every decision should take into account the influence of the Survival Natural Force on the outcome of what is being planned. To make a decision of this magnitude, you need all the data available. You must also listen to your emotions and the opinions of others concerning the potential impact of the decision. Everyone who is part of the decision-making process should understand both the benefits and the risks involved.

In the simplest of terms, the question to be asked is "What influence, either supportive or adverse, might these actions or decisions have on the ultimate survival of the organization?" Before making any major decision that could have an impact on the Survival Natural Force, this question must be thoroughly explored and the potential risks communicated to all stakeholders. Risks are fine and often absolutely necessary, but they must also be understood before major decisions are made.

Behavior and the Natural Forces

Understanding the reasons for the existence of all the Natural Forces is critical to managing them effectively. The better you are able to really understand the driving force behind people's behaviors, the better you will be able to respond to their needs.

Consider a situation in which a supervisor learns that a top-performing employee is interviewing for a job with a competitor. A supervisor might adopt either one of the two following approaches. Read the dialogue between the supervisor and the employee and think about how an understanding of Natural Forces could affect the final result. In addition, consider how each approach might lead to a different outcome.

APPROACH A

Supervisor: I understand that you are interviewing with XYZ Company. Why would you want to do that? You know how they do business. Besides, I want to remind you that you signed confidentiality agreements with us when we hired you several years ago. We will take you and XYZ to court if you violate any of these agreements.

Employee: I have already talked to XYZ's attorneys and there is no problem with my confidentiality agreements. I'm not going to be working in any areas that will represent a conflict of interest with these agreements before they expire. I might as well give you my notice now. My last day will be the 15th of the month.

Supervisor: No, your last day will be today.

APPROACH B

Supervisor: I heard that you were talking to XYZ Company. Are you thinking about leaving us? We'd be sorry to see you go. We think you have a great future with our company, and we really like the work you've been doing. What's going on?

Employee: Yes, I've talked to them. I guess, to answer your question, I'm actually surprised to hear you say that I have a good future here. To be honest, I'd rather stay with this company, but I'm concerned about my future and job security. There are so many cutbacks going on right now that I'm just not sure where I stand. XYZ has made a commitment to me concerning job security that is very attractive.

Supervisor: Oh, I'm beginning to understand. What if we were to make the same commitment concerning your future with our company? Would you be willing to stay with us?

Employee: Yes.

Obviously, these two approaches yielded very different results. The first demonstrated no sensitivity toward the employee. It did nothing to increase the manager's understanding of the situation or get to the root cause of the problem, which was job security. By taking the first approach, the manager simply sped up the termination process. And the bottom line was that the company lost a valuable employee to a competitor.

In the second example, the manager took a different approach. Instead of attacking the situation using aggressive tactics, the manager began to probe to find out the real reason behind the employee's possible job change. The manager set the stage for discovering this information by showing some sensitivity to the reasons for the employee's actions and steering the dialogue in that direction. If a company is experiencing major cutbacks, as was the case in this circumstance, managers should be aware of the impact this could have on even those who are not being tapped on the shoulder for unannounced meetings in the boss's office at 9:00 A.M. This is the proactive approach to managing Natural Forces.

The manager in the first scenario allowed this Natural Force to work against the company and lost control of the situation. In the second example, the manager used this Natural Force to avoid the loss of a valuable contributor. Rather than considering an employee's interest in going to a competitor as an act equivalent to corporate treason, consider such a move in terms of this Natural Force. Once you understand it as a survival issue, you will be in a better position to deal effectively with the situation.

Influence of the Survival Force

I hope you have seen just how powerful a force survival can be for both employees and the organization. It can change the structure and very nature of even the largest and most successful organizations. The Survival Force presents itself in both real and perceived forms, either of which can be extremely powerful.

Threats to survival will destroy any individual's sense of security. As with a starving man searching for food, there will be only one thing on an employee's mind when his or her security is in jeopardy. There can be no real growth and development until this Natural Force is adequately addressed. This is not to say that you could or even should eliminate all threats to security in your organization. The realities of survival should always be at least in the back of people's minds even during the most successful of times. However, employees at all levels of the organization need to believe that they can work toward a sense of security and stability. They need to feel that they have some control over their careers and futures. If their current situation is threatening their survival, they must understand how to deal with it. Employees will be willing to support virtually any plan that helps assure their future and that of the organization, as long as they understand it. The first challenge of any crisis management initiative is to channel this Natural Force of Survival into productive and corrective actions that will prevent the problem from recurring again and again.

In order for any organization to move forward, this essential Natural Force must be reckoned with and understood. People as well as organizations value survival above any other need. Its importance is often taken for granted during good times, and its true meaning is usually fully comprehended only in its absence. Similarly, employees tend to not fully appreciate their jobs until they are gone, and organizations often take for granted the contributions of their workers.

Survival is a force that never truly goes away and can return to center stage at any time. There is no immunity to this force. Even the most powerful and successful organizations and people can't escape it. Even if you are riding the wave of prosperity during the longest economic boom in decades, you are always subject to the Natural Force of Survival, which can arrive at any moment with little or no notice. Survival is indeed an equal opportunity Natural Force.

The following chart is a quick reference for the Survival Natural Force. It provides examples of ways to better manage or influence this force, specific actions or programs you might implement, and the impact these actions could have on employees.

Quick Reference for the Survival Natural Force

INFLUENCE ON NATURAL FORCE	MANAGEMENT ACTIONS	IMPACT ON EMPLOYEES
Employee development programs	Establish promotion schedules, management development programs, salary merit reviews.	Enhances employees' sense of security.
Training and development	Provide both job function and management development training programs for employees.	Improves job skills, knowledge, and motivation.
Business updates	Hold regular business update meetings for all employees.	Increases understanding of current business conditions and their impact on the organization.
Confidentiality agreements	Have all employees sign confidentiality agreements and explain why information must be restricted.	Increases understanding of the sensitivity of certain information.
Reorganizations/ realignments	Announce these changes as quickly as possible. Ensure understanding of new reporting relationships and responsibilities.	Increases understanding of new responsibilities and reporting relationships and their impact on employees.
Contracts	Provide employment contracts for as many levels of employees as possible.	Clarifies the commitments the company has made to the employees.
Contingency plans	Develop and communicate business contingency plans to all employees.	Lets employees know what to expect if certain circumstances develop.
Employment market	Let employees know their value to the organization. Be aware of incentives that competitors might offer to lure employees away. Provide outplacement services when reducing the workforce.	Enables employees to explore other employment opportunities if necessary and understand their market value.
Political issues	Develop educational programs to share the current political issues important to the organization.	Increases awareness of the political issues of the day that could affect the organization and employees' jobs.
International issues	Provide information to employees concerning the organization's position on international issues and how it might affect their jobs.	Shows employees how international issues may influence their jobs and ultimately their security.
Labor contracts	Ensure that employees understand the benefits the contract provides and the extent to which their security can be contractually guaranteed.	Clarifies how much security a labor contract may or may not be able to provide.

Change

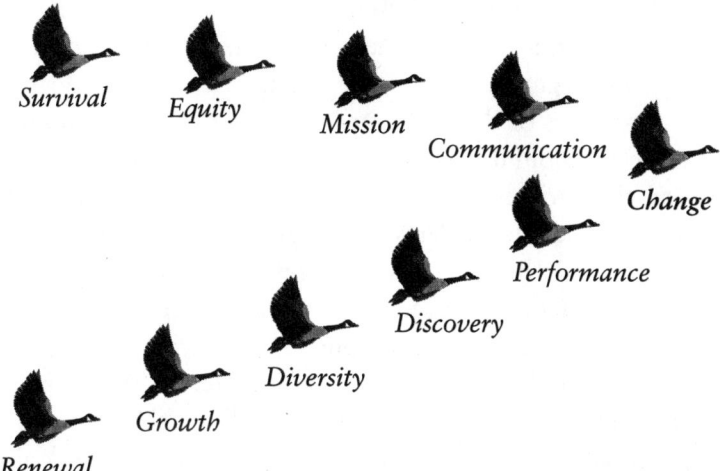

Survival Equity Mission Communication Change Performance Discovery Diversity Growth Renewal

LAWS OF THE CHANGE NATURAL FORCE

• Change can involve a paradigm shift.

• Without change, there would be no progress.

• Adapting to change is essential for survival.

• Change is not the enemy.

• Change must be anticipated.

Given a choice, most people would elect to keep things pretty much the same, particularly when it comes to their jobs. Change takes us out of our comfort zones and away from the safe and familiar. It creates strange new ways of doing things and forces us into processes that we may know nothing about or with which we have little expertise. This can be very scary. Change comes to all organizations, like it or not. It usually arrives before everyone is ready. There is often nothing particularly wrong with current conditions; it's just that something new has come onto the scene. Something that changes everything.

Change Can Involve a Paradigm Shift

In his book *Future Edge,* Joel Barker (1992) defines a *paradigm* as a set of rules and regulations (written or unwritten) that does two things: (1) establishes or defines boundaries, and (2) tells you how to behave inside the boundaries in order to be successful. Success is measured by the problems you solve using those rules and regulations. Paradigms become the lenses through which we see the world. If something doesn't fit this view, it is rejected, even though there might be a great deal of evidence and many reasons for its acceptance.

Barker uses the dramatic example of the Swiss watch-making industry in 1967 to help explain this principle. At that time, the Swiss dominated the watch market. Their skill at making the finest mainspring watches of the day was world renowned. But think about how many people wear this type of watch today. You would probably be hard-pressed to find anyone with a watch with a mainspring and jewel movement on his or her wrist. Why? Because, as Barker explains, a paradigm shift occurred with the introduction of the digital quartz watch in the late 1960s.

Who do you think invented this new product that changed the entire watch industry forever? As Barker points out, you might be surprised to learn that it was the Swiss, who didn't realize its significance. After all, it didn't fit their 1967 paradigm of how a watch should operate. It didn't have a mainspring. It didn't even tick. How could such an invention ever evolve into the next generation of watches that would be worn the world over? So convinced were they that there wasn't anything really significant about the quartz watch that they didn't even bother to protect it from competitors. Companies such as Texas Instruments and Seiko took one look, and the rest is now part of timekeeping history.

An important lesson here, as Barker explains, is that there wasn't really anything wrong with the type of watch that was standard at the time of the paradigm shift. As a matter of fact, these watches worked quite nicely. Swiss watches were synonymous with quality. A Swiss-made jewel-movement watch even became a status symbol. But the new quartz watches were both cheaper to produce and significantly more accurate than the old watches. This caused a paradigm shift in watch making that changed the industry forever. Paradigm shifts are a distinct form of change in that they have the potential to alter the natural order of things.

Without Change, There Would Be No Progress

Change is one Natural Force that is constantly eroding the status quo in organizations. You can resist change, but you will be fighting a losing battle. Change is a necessity—without it, there could be no progress.

Progress is actually a series of paradigm shifts that occur over time, with each shift changing the way we do business. According to Barker, everything goes back to zero when a paradigm shift occurs. Organizations and their systems and products all go through evolutions similar to the life cycle.

Think about some of the other major paradigm shifts of the past century. What do you think it must have been like when new inventions such as the railroad, automobile, telephone, or airplane—just to name a few—were introduced and dramatically changed people's lives? You can be sure that many people resisted each of these marvelous new discoveries. They probably had financial or emotional investments (or both) in the old paradigms. Part of the problem is that paradigm shifts are not always clean breaks with the past. Lingering doubts and transitional problems may still exist, thus feeding the uncertainty of the skeptics as well as of the believers.

Technology doesn't always keep up with paradigm-shifting ideas, which causes other setbacks and delays in evolutionary change. Eventually, though, technology catches up and propels change ahead even faster. Cellular phones, for example, originally didn't provide the same clarity as corded phones did, and people also worried about the security of conversations broadcast over the airwaves. Today, due to advances in technology, cell phones are commonplace. Seeing this phenomenon, you may wonder how we managed before we had cell phones. The answer is that because we did not realize we were missing anything, we did just fine. This is the effect of a paradigm shift. It changes our expectations, our habits, and ultimately our lives. This change is usually thought to be an improvement; however, there is generally a price to pay with the introduction of anything new. In this case, it might be that increased accessibility makes it difficult to get away from work. However, the cost may be greatly outweighed by the benefits, for example, by the fact that mobile phones allow you to stay in touch with other family members. All change must be measured in terms of its costs and its benefits. In the early stages of change, people tend to focus on the costs. As the changes become institutionalized, the benefits are more clearly recognized.

There is a reason for every change. It may address some need or failing in the old system that set the stage for the new paradigm. Accepting change requires this level of understanding so that we can see its true benefits and potential.

Adapting to Change Is Essential for Survival

Change is perhaps the most constant Natural Force that exists. The power of change must be harnessed in order to align the organization's goals with the enormous and unrelenting momentum of change. Think about the arrival of the Internet on the business scene just a few years ago. It represented a major sea change in the way the world communicated and conducted transactions. What if an organization had tried to resist this change? What do you think its fate would have been? Every organization must keep up with the pace of change or be steamrolled by its arrival.

Although cyclical downturns in the economy and in NASDAQ stock prices make skeptics of even the most futuristic thinkers in an organization, you don't have to be a fortune-teller to predict the role of technology in the future. The only question is how fast these changes will come. Learning to adapt to change is essential for both organizations and employees.

Change Is Not the Enemy

One of the problems with change is that people are constantly going around saying negative things about it. No wonder it gets such a bad rap. Think about the last time you said something positive about change. Chances are that it has been a while. In order to better manage this Natural Force, you must begin to look at it differently. Change is not really your enemy. It doesn't have anything against you personally. It is just trying to perform its function, which is to sustain progress in the world. And it does its job quite well. The Natural Force of Change is much bigger than you or anyone else in your organization.

Managers often refuse to recognize that change is under way in their organizations, for change makes them feel that they aren't in control in their areas of responsibility and authority. These feelings cause them to resist change. This syndrome occurs on all levels, from the chairman down to the production worker. People often respond to change with statements like "I'm never going to go along with that," or "Don't they understand that's not the way we do things around here?" However, you would be well advised to avoid making such statements and tying your future to people who express similar sentiments, for these statements are evidence that an individual is a *change anchor*. A change anchor is someone who becomes a drag on the organization. Anchors slow down an organization's development and progress. Anchors do have a practical purpose in life—but only if you want to stand still, a state in which most organizations today would prefer not to find themselves. What do you do if you find that there is an anchor slowing down your progress? The quickest solution is to cut it loose. Gaining a reputation as an anchor is certainly not the way to achieve job security, much less a promising career, within your organization.

Change Must Be Anticipated

Change is a patient Natural Force. It can come suddenly, as was the case with the dot-com industry's abrupt arrival. When paradigm-shifting change arrives on the scene, awareness is suddenly not a problem. Everyone is talking about the change and its effects on their lives and futures. But change can also occur like the steady drip that eventually wears away rock and cuts canyons through mountains.

When it creeps in as if it is sneaking in the back door, it can be more problematic.

Slow changes—what we call *blips*—are the ones that cause the most difficulty when it comes to provoking appropriate responses. A popular business metaphor today is the radar screen that forecasts changes in organizations. "We need to get that on our radar screen" is often heard when people are considering something new during strategic planning meetings and reviews. A blip on a radar screen is just what it sounds like. It is a momentary indication that something has been detected, which disappears as quickly as it appeared. Blips are easy to dismiss and ignore. Maybe it was just some kind of false signal or electrical interference, one might surmise. In aviation, a blip might be thought of as nothing more than a flock of birds flying across the sky—such was the interpretation of a blip on a radar screen that was seen heading toward Pearl Harbor on December 7, 1941.

It is important to recognize blips on the organizational radar screen for what they really represent. These blips may be simply static or abnormalities on the business scene—but not always. Most events give us some kind of forewarning, even if we don't always recognize the signs. It is not until later that we think back and say to ourselves, "You know, that did strike me as very unusual, but I didn't really give it much thought at the time." A blip might be an indication that a major change or paradigm shift is on the way. In Barker's terms, it might be the first indication that the current paradigm is no longer effective at solving today's problems. However, a blip can be much more subtle. It might be a comment, an unusual response, a question, a phone message left on your desk that you file away, meaning to return the call at a later time. It might be something you see on the back pages of the morning newspaper. One of the most important skills of a manager or leader in an organization is the ability to recognize blips. Unfortunately, change always seems to arrive before anyone is really ready for it. People as well as organizations are not prepared for change because they are often quite satisfied with the status quo. Anticipating change is one of an organization's main challenges.

Rules for Change Agents

Contrary to what your emotions may be telling you when change is introduced into your organization, resisting it is not your best strategy. In today's dynamic business environment, organizations need *change agents*. A change agent is the polar opposite of a change anchor. Change agents help in the implementation of change. They welcome rather than resist it. Change agents probably experience the same emotions about change that anchors do, but they don't give in to the urge to resist. Remember, you will ultimately be judged not by how much you argued against the change or tried to resist it but by what you did to aid in its implementation. Going around telling everyone that you think a change is stupid will only label you as a change anchor. This is not a career-enhancing strategy for any manager or supervisor.

If you truly want to be a change agent in your organization, there are a number of rules that you should understand and incorporate into your management philosophy and style. Following these rules can help you avoid being constantly controlled by this Natural Force and instead will allow you to manage change more effectively. Even if some or perhaps all of these rules seem completely foreign to your management style or propensities, don't panic. Remember the Natural Force we are talking about here—change. You, too, can change. It is within your control and ability to make the transformation from being a change anchor (if that's what you are today) to a change agent. Even if you would describe yourself as more of a change agent than an anchor, these rules can help you become a better manager of the Natural Force of Change.

Understand What You Are Changing

You must first understand the old system before you introduce a new one. You do this not so much to question the need for change (that is probably a given at this point if you are even considering a change) but to understand why the old system worked or didn't work, for there are probably other, more subtle, forces at work that supported the old system and made it tick. You need to understand these forces in order to ensure that whatever you introduce is not doomed to failure because important factors are missing. Without this knowledge, you could be walking into a minefield without even realizing these dangers exist. To make the scenario even worse, there could be change anchors watching as you stumble into these land mines, all the while saying smugly to one another that they knew the change you introduced was never going to work.

Taking a systemic approach helps you understand the infrastructure that is necessary to support change. This infrastructure may include many factors, both tangible and intangible, such as computer systems, technology, resource allocation, technical expertise, communications, administrative services, and even political clout, just to name a few. If you strip away any of the elements that made the old system function, you may be creating a scenario for disaster. This is not to say that some or possibly even all the factors supporting the current system need to be addressed or eliminated before real change can occur. Rather, before you knock the pegs out from under the current system, you need replacements that will serve the purpose better. Many efforts to create paradigm-shifting change in organizations have failed because this step was not thoroughly thought out or even considered.

An excellent example of the inability to understand the current system when introducing change occurred in the 1990s. At the time, many organizations began implementing the concepts of empowerment and teamwork in the workplace. These concepts essentially involved moving decision making and problem solving to the lowest possible organizational levels. The goal of these management philosophies was to empower those who worked closest to the problems to make better and quicker decisions, eliminating obstacles and enabling the operation to run more effectively and efficiently. This sounds like a worthwhile objective, but a number of organizational realities may not have been considered.

One of the first requirements in a systemic approach to introducing a major change is to identify which jobs will be most affected. The supervisors of employees who were empowered with new decision-making responsibilities felt greatly threatened. The dialogue between supervisors and managers as these concepts were introduced could have gone something like this:

Supervisor: Let me see if I understand this new system you're introducing. You're going to give the people who work for me the decision-making and problem-solving authority that has been a major part of my job all these years. If my employees are going to be doing my job, what's my role going to be?

Manager: Well, I guess that is a good question, and we really haven't thought about it yet. I don't know what your new role will be, but we'll let you know as soon as we figure it out. We'll get back to you on this issue. Trust us—this will be a much better system for everyone. You'll really like it, you'll see.

Reading this dialogue, you might be thinking that the answer to this problem is relatively simple. All you have to do is either get rid of the supervisors (which is what many organizations mistakenly rushed to do) or determine their future roles in the organization (a much more effective approach).

Either solution requires a complete understanding of the effect of these changes on the entire organization. Rushing to eliminate the supervisory function can result in *reckless empowerment,* which implies that you have given responsibility and authority to employees before they are ready. This can have disastrous results and has been responsible for ending many empowerment initiatives in organizations. Employees became upset because they were being asked to accept responsibility for areas in which they weren't properly trained or prepared to perform; supervisors felt they were still being held accountable yet no longer had any control. Simply eliminating supervisors often left gaps that untrained or poorly prepared employees were unable to fill. Employees also felt they weren't being fairly compensated for their increased responsibilities (see chapter 5).

There is no doubt that the introduction of new management philosophies and systems such as empowerment can bring much needed change into organizations and result in dramatically improved performance, but you must understand exactly what you are changing and consider as many variables as possible. If you were participating in the dialogue above, you would need to be able to answer the supervisor's question "What's my role going to be?" before you began to implement this change. Otherwise, you would in essence be going forward under the operational philosophy of "ready, fire, and aim." It works a lot better if you identify your target beforehand.

Seek Advice from Unconventional Sources

Before former first lady Hillary Clinton began her successful campaign to become a United States senator, she went on what was called a listening tour of New York State. Her purpose was reportedly to listen to what the people of New York had to say concerning her chances of being elected their next senator. Based on the results, it appears that what Senator Clinton heard during this tour gave her the justification and motivation to launch a full-fledged campaign and seek this major career change. Maybe you need to go on a listening tour of your organization.

The answers aren't always so easy to find. You have to search for them, often from unconventional sources and in unusual places. You might be surprised by how much you can learn by just listening to others. All the answers are not always at the top of the organization. Neither are all the brains. Just as top management tends to seriously underestimate employees' ability to understand when their survival is as risk, it also fails to recognize the vast amount of untapped knowledge that exists in the workforce. Employees at all levels of the organization can be extremely valuable sources of information and advice on how to manage change. From their experience, they know what will work and what won't. You don't have to invest huge amounts of money to confirm what they could tell you for free; instead, you can tap relatively easily into this huge reservoir of knowledge. All you have to do is ask. Your employees will let you know whether or not your idea is a good one and how to make it work if it is.

In addition, those who deal with your organization on a regular basis may also be a valuable source of information. Your suppliers, customers, vendors, and even service people have valuable insights and information about your organization—and they can be yours just by asking and listening to what they have to say. These "outsiders" see the organization from a different perspective than you as a manager do. They don't have the same emotional or career investments in the current structure or operations. They may be biased according to their own self-interests and roles, but this typically is pretty easy to see. All they really know is what they observe. They are not as enmeshed in the political processes of your organization, which puts them in a unique position to see the truth about your company. They may be questioning why you do certain things that really don't make sense to them, based on their experiences doing business with other organizations. Outsiders also hear things from within your company that you don't have the chance to hear. They can be a safe ear for employees who need to vent their frustrations about how things are being done and what needs to change. They may be the only ones who are listening to some of your employees' best ideas about how to improve your organization.

The problem is that we tend to go to the same sources for information and advice on managing change. If something worked for us in the past, we generally go back to that source for guidance. If your stockbroker told you to move all your investments into high-technology stocks in the late 1990s, by the beginning of 2000 you would have thought he was a financial genius. Why would you ever leave that brokerage firm for an investment counselor who didn't believe the high-tech boom would continue for at least the rest of the first decade of the new millennium? This is the problem with seeking advice about change. People sometimes tell you things you don't want to hear or believe. It is easy to dismiss information that doesn't fit your current view or paradigm of the world, but obviously things do change. The dot-com industry crash wasn't really all that hard to see coming and was predicted by many financial analysts. All you had to do was listen and accept the bad news that the high-tech bubble was about to burst, even though you may not have wanted to believe your ears.

Reinvent the Wheel

"Let's not reinvent the wheel" is a common expression in business today, meaning that what is needed is already available and doesn't have to be created again. Granted that there certainly are times when this is true, this overall philosophy can be very stifling to new ideas. After all, if the wheel didn't need reinvention, why are there so many variations of this device? It's important to challenge the institutionalized fixtures in your organization, those "wheels" that are generally perceived as part of the established culture of the organization.

To give you fair warning, you should know that your efforts to change institutionalized processes, procedures, methods, and practices will be met with a heavy barrage of organized resistance. You will be given long lectures about the history, background, and importance of these institutionalized practices. You might even find yourself in your boss's office—meaning you have done something either very good or very bad. In this situation, it is actually a little of both. What you are trying to do is really a very good thing for the organization, but people don't realize it yet. It is a little like taking a spoonful of bad-tasting medicine.

There is one thing to be said about being a reinventor of the wheel—it takes guts. You need the courage of your convictions to suggest changing things that are considered sacred to the organization. Someone once said that *approach* has everything to do with success, and it is certainly true in this case. How you introduce this type of change, as well as how flexible you can be in your efforts, will have a huge effect on the final result. Tread carefully, but make your arguments for change heard; most of all, have patience. It probably took many years for these types of institutionalized policies and practices to develop, so don't expect them to be abandoned overnight.

Know When to Give Up

There are times when you simply have to stop trying to make something work if it is not worth the cost and effort of your investment. Disengaging from a goal into which you have poured your heart and soul for perhaps years can be very hard to do. Projects of this type take on a life of their own. They begin to define a person's career. When this happens, beware. As this Natural Force constantly reminds us, things can change dramatically in an instant. If a paradigm shift occurs, all the rules will be different. You must remain as flexible as possible concerning change. When it is time to move on, move on. Hanging on too long to plans that are obviously not going to produce the expected results will only cause others to perceive you as a change anchor. Stop perpetuating failure because of the investments you've made in a project or process, even if you have the political influence and support to keep the funding coming.

Provide the Resources Needed for Change

What gets resources gets accomplished in organizations. Given adequate money, time, and support, you can make just about any project at least moderately successful or can portray it as such. The more important question is, Should that project or process be funded? Are you sponsoring funding for the right things? You may need to take a closer look at what you are doing with your resources. Are you expecting your most important goals to be accomplished without the necessary resources? Are they becoming the "poor cousins" of your organization's goals? You must ensure that you are providing the necessary resources for those projects and processes that are the real drivers for change in your organization. Otherwise, they may not happen.

The bottom line is this—unless you are providing the resources to sustain change in your organization, you may unwittingly be playing the role of a change anchor. Paying lip service to a desired change isn't always enough to make it happen. You have to put your money where your mouth is. Speeches and memos are one thing, but people don't really take you seriously unless they see something more tangible (like money) put into the action plan.

Change the Metrics

A corollary to "what gets resources gets accomplished" is "what gets measured gets noticed." People do pay closer attention to what is measured.

As a manager, one of your most powerful influences over others is in determining what your employees are to report. If you hold someone accountable for a certain performance measure, you can be sure that person will be doing everything in his or her power to give you the numbers you want to see. If you really want to change behaviors, you must recognize progress made toward these performance measures. This is called *shaping behavior*. You shape behavior by recognizing even incremental improvements and letting the individual know that he or she is on the right track. Recognition doesn't have to be something tangible. Just acknowledging that you are aware of these improvements can have a tremendous effect in motivating the person to continue on this positive track. Recognition can take the form of a passing comment or a note on a report that comes across your desk and is sent back to the employee. If you ignore the things that people have worked hardest to accomplish and recognize those they feel are meaningless, you will accomplish little. Find out what people are doing that is driving change in your organization and give them the recognition and reinforcement they deserve.

Management's failure to understand this concept is one of the main reasons hourly employees in particular are often mistrustful. Think about it from their perspective. These employees come to work each day and do essentially the same thing. They perform their jobs as they were trained and instructed to do until they are told to do something different. They become quite proficient in their duties, which they perform repetitively day after day. Their performance is measured for each shift in order to compare and report productivity in some manner, but a number of variables undoubtedly affect productivity during the shift, such as machine run time, raw materials, other processes, and product specifications. The point is that the workers are most likely hardworking and diligent on each shift, but the process variables that make a difference in performance are usually out of their control. Let's say, for example, that during one reporting period the workers' production ends up being very high, and, in an attempt to reinforce the desirability of this result and encourage workers to duplicate their success, management offers recognition in the form of a gift presented to everyone. On another occasion, when the production indexes are very low, stern words are spoken or warnings are issued that this trend must not continue. The employee might say, "I don't get it. I come in here and do the same thing every day. One day they say I'm doing a great job, and the next they're kicking me in the behind. I wish they'd make up their minds!"

Workers may be confused because they believe they are doing essentially the same thing during productive as well as unproductive time periods. What you are actually reinforcing or punishing is *process variation,* and employees will not be able to see the connection between their behaviors and management's rewards or disapproval. Conversely, when linked to a clearly understood cause-and-effect relationship, rewarding employees for successful results can create more positive change than perhaps any other action you could take as a manager.

Just as rewards reinforce desired behaviors, misapplied punishment may extinguish these same behaviors. Does your organization punish sincere attempts to be successful even if the goals are not met? In other words, do you punish failure? If you do, it is a safe bet that there will be little risk taking in your organization. This is another good reason to look at both behaviors and results when you study the metrics that are driving change in your organization.

Stop Feeding Instant Gratification

"I want it now!" is the cry of most executives today, feeling pressure from their stockholders and subsequently from boards of directors clamoring for their heads if they don't meet next quarter's financial goals. This mind-set squashes more strategic planning than perhaps anything else in business today. The fallout from these management tantrums costs organizations huge bucks in the long run. Of course, the problem with this limited vision is that without longer-range investments, you will never reap the corresponding rewards. Japanese companies tend to have a competitive advantage over their American counterparts in this area. They generally have much more realistic expectations for short-term returns and focus more on long-range goals. Eventually, these investments do come to fruition and, by their very nature, have the potential to produce more systemic improvements than does an isolated instant goal.

A true champion of change looks at both immediate and longer-range goals when making decisions. In some situations, you must forgo short-term gains in order to set the stage for future success. You need to have the courage of your convictions so that you will be able to weather the top-level management storms created by this type of decision making. Remember, change is a powerful Natural Force. Trying to block its arrival is a battle you cannot win. You may be able to manipulate several variables and thus squeeze some additional profits out of a process or situation that has run its course, but these gains won't last long. Sooner or later, the natural order of things will assert itself in your organizational world. Without planning strategically for these changes, you could find yourself completely at the mercy of this Natural Force. Stop giving in to your urge for instant gratification, and prepare for tomorrow's changes. They will be here sooner than you think. You might have to battle intense resistance, but if you are successful, you will ultimately be perceived as a change agent if not the hero who saved the day for the organization.

Follow Decision-Making Trails

A decision-making trail leads to the real decision makers in the organization. When you follow these trails, you may be surprised at where you end up. The people you have assumed to be the decision makers may not be making the calls after all. Perhaps the process occurs at levels that are higher, or even lower, than you expected or would consciously have authorized.

An important decision-making process might have been delegated inadvertently to a lower level, where the person responsible may not have a clue as to the potential consequences of each decision. For example, a dispatcher might be sending out deliveries based on factors other than the customers' needs because nobody bothered to explain shipment priorities to him. Conversely, decisions might be made at unexpectedly higher levels, particularly if you have a controlling executive calling the shots. Learning who makes decisions in an organization and how tells you where you really need to go to make change happen. Trying to create change at other levels will only lead you into an organizational maze. So put on your hiking boots and hit the decision-making trail. Start by asking questions about who is involved in the approval process for whatever decisions you are investigating. This will take you to the heart and soul of change in your organization.

Stop Analysis to Paralysis

In too many organizations, too many people want too many numbers before they even begin to consider making anything that resembles a decision. This overanalysis can paralyze an organization when action is what is really needed. While the organization is painstakingly contemplating a decision, competitors may already have implemented change and be reaping its rewards. By the time the analysis is completed and a decision is finally made, it may all be for naught. It may be too late. The window of opportunity is usually open for but a brief moment before being quickly nailed shut again. These kinds of organizations are slow to catch on, and when something new appears on the horizon, they begin the whole ritual again, questioning the wisdom of trying to make up for their previous indecision by jumping into the current situation too quickly. And so the cycle continues. By the time they decide to make their move, so has everyone else. This leaves them no choice but to rely on some other factor for success. Perhaps it is excellent customer service or technological development, but it certainly will not be responsiveness to market demands.

If this is the mind-set in your organization, you need to help change this organizational culture, for it puts you at an immediate disadvantage compared to competitors who are more responsive to the need for change. Cultural change does not come easy and can seem as powerful as a Natural Force in itself, but it must be addressed. Just as they are for any other business deliverable, organizational leaders should be accountable for cultural change. They need to attack it in the same way they would any other ambitious business goal. Change must become a top priority of the organization and should be regularly reviewed at executive-level meetings. If this does not happen, the organization will continue this cycle of analysis to paralysis, missing out on more and more opportunities and wondering why the competition always seems to be ahead of the game.

Admit That You Dislike Change As Much As Anyone Else

This is nothing to be ashamed of. Regardless of what people say, they don't much like change either. The challenge is to understand your human frailties concerning change, and the most important thing is to not let these feelings cloud your judgment. Don't make excuses for avoiding change based on illogical rationales or distorted facts. This will only magnify the problems that come with trying to resist this Natural Force. Remember, it's bigger than you or anyone else in your organization. You can't fight it or pretend it's not there. You need to be honest with your emotions concerning change and deal with them in a positive and proactive way.

Being frank about your misgivings will not label you as a change anchor but will actually do the reverse. By admitting your true feelings about change, you help others get in touch with their own fears and concerns. As in dealing with any other behaviorally based problem, this is the first step toward recovery. By your example, you can help others in the organization make the transformation from change anchors to change agents, which will eventually have a tremendous impact on bottom-line results. As Darwin discovered, those who are most adaptable are most likely to survive and thrive in the future.

Leading Change

Peter Senge (1990), the well-known organization development expert and successful author, describes in his popular book *The Fifth Discipline: The Art and Practice of the Learning Organization* the challenges faced by organizations confronted with this Natural Force. Senge explains that an organization must continually expand its capacity to create its future. The way to achieve this objective is through what he describes as "systems thinking," which involves seeing relationships in the organization rather than linear cause-and-effect chains. You need to look for processes of change, not snapshots or isolated events that are causing problems. The art of systems thinking lies in seeing through complexity to the underlying structures generating change.

The problem with many organizations is that they are too leader dependent. The entire system is designed around the strength of the top executive. Everything works wonderfully as long as this leader is at the head of the board of directors' conference table, controlling every major (and minor) organizational decision. But what happens when this leader is gone or can no longer effectively lead the organization?

Today's effective leaders not only react to change in a decisive manner but create systems designed to anticipate and respond to future change. This is the true function of a visionary leader—to help others see what lies ahead and prepare for the inevitable changes of the future. By preparing for change, you harness the power of this Natural Force so that all its energy propels you toward meeting your goals. Moving in the direction of change may seem effortless and natural, while resisting this Natural Force can be extraordinarily destructive to an organization.

The companies most successful in the future will be those whose current leaders judge their performance not by what they accomplished personally while at the helm but by how well they prepared their organizations to respond to change in the future. This is perhaps the greatest legacy of any leader.

The following chart is a quick reference for the Change Natural Force. It provides examples of ways to better manage or influence this force, specific actions or programs you might implement, and the impact these actions could have on employees.

Quick Reference for the Change Natural Force		
INFLUENCE ON NATURAL FORCE	MANAGEMENT ACTIONS	IMPACT ON EMPLOYEES
Reorganizations	Design a new organization to be more responsive to change.	Helps make change successful.
Policy changes	Design policies that can be adapted to change.	Increases employees' understanding of how the new rules will affect them.
New leadership	Guide change so that it proceeds smoothly and is more accepted by the organization.	Increases acceptance of and adjustment to change.
New products/ services	Study the organizational impact of new products or services.	Creates significant job change.
Economic shifts	Deal with changes caused by economic shifts.	Makes people feel like victims of economic cycles, with frequent layoffs and rehires.
Technological advances	Factor technological advances into strategic planning.	Creates need to understand how to utilize new technology to the company's advantage.
New business plans	Adapt to changes caused by new business strategies and plans.	Creates need to understand new business plans.
Acquisitions	Blend different corporate cultures and communicate the outcome to employees.	Models how to adapt to the new culture.
Divestitures	Keep everyone informed as divestitures begin to develop.	Creates need to understand each stage of the process and how the changes will affect jobs.
Laws/policies/ regulations	Communicate the effect on the organization and any changes that may result.	Creates need to understand the new rules and how to comply with them.
New administrations	Communicate all planned changes.	Increases desire to be kept informed of resulting changes.
Turnover	Understand the reasons for turnover and develop strategies to reduce its impact on the organization.	Increases responsibility of survivors.

Communication

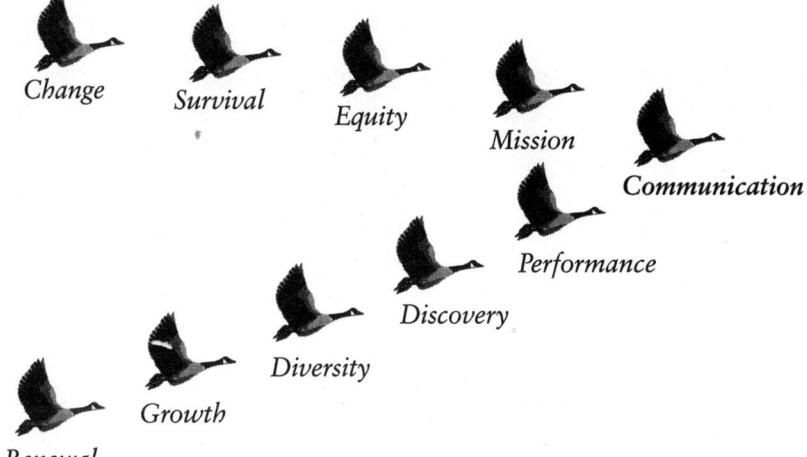

Change · Survival · Equity · Mission · Communication · Performance · Discovery · Diversity · Growth · Renewal

LAWS OF THE COMMUNICATION
NATURAL FORCE

- Communication is the key to solving problems.

- Poor communication is often the symptom, not the problem.

- Communication is a powerful need.

- Everybody loves a rumor.

- Effective leadership requires effective communication.

Establishing effective communication can be an elusive goal for any organization. Just when you think you have achieved it, a new communication breakdown surfaces. The Communication Natural Force can have a significant impact on your organization's ability to operate efficiently and effectively. Your employees will judge you as much by your skill as a communicator as by any other criterion.

Communication Is the Key to Solving Problems

Establishing better communication is the solution to virtually every organizational problem. If you doubt that this is really the case (and you would be in good company), ask yourself this question: Can I think of a problem at work or even in my personal life that wasn't created or solved on some level by communication? Over the course of many years, a successful management consultant asked this question of every group with which he worked. His clients included companies both large and small, in industries that ranged from high technology to basic labor, public- and private-sector organizations, and employees at all levels. Not once did anyone give him an example of a problem that didn't link back to communication in some significant manner.

Poor Communication Is Often the Symptom, Not the Problem

Poor communication is most often a symptom of ineffective management and other organizational problems and is not the problem itself. The root cause of poor communication may lie deep within the organization, and until it is addressed, effective communication may not be possible. To address only an organization's communication problems is like treating the symptoms but not the cause of the disease. However, improving communication should definitely be part of the solution; anything you do to correct the problems in your organization must be communicated effectively. Ignoring this powerful Natural Force will doom any resolution process.

Communication Is a Powerful Need

Don't ever underestimate the power of communication. People will always find a way to communicate. Children pass notes behind the teacher's back to communicate during class when they are supposed to be listening to the lesson. Prisoners of war captured by the North Vietnamese developed a system that involved tapping out coded messages through the walls of their cells.

Employees develop informal but extremely effective networks for disseminating information about what is going on in the company. Communication can slip through even the tiniest cracks in your organization. Employees will see through any attempt to divert attention from a topic that you prefer not to discuss. They will ask you the most stinging questions, aimed with pinpoint accuracy to land squarely on the truth. They will not be satisfied with anything less than communication conducted at the highest level, and even then they may still complain that they aren't receiving enough information.

Communication is also essential to the organization as a whole. It is an extremely powerful force that can't be stopped. Information will be communicated within the organization by one means or another. If management creates a void in communication, employees will fill it. That is why it is so vitally important to communicate information concerning both the current situation and the future business outlook. Employees on all levels need to know how they are doing individually and as an organization. Without effective communication and feedback, the organization will be left with nothing but speculation. This is why it is so difficult to keep confidential information confidential. Doing so defies this Natural Force.

Everybody Loves a Rumor

We as human beings have a tremendous innate drive to seek information. In organizations, this drive usually manifests itself in the form of the rumor mill, a tremendously powerful force that cannot be stopped by any management order or effort. Everybody loves a rumor, and virtually everyone participates in spreading them. The only way to kill the rumor mill (or, more realistically, wound it!) is to starve it. You do this by beating it to the punch. This means sharing information openly from the beginning. One of the greatest fallacies regarding management is that it has the ability to keep confidential information confidential.

The rumor mill has obvious limitations as a reliable communication source. You are likely familiar with the childhood game of "telephone."

In this game, the first child whispers a message to the second child, and the message is repeated down the line until the last child announces his or her version of the message—which usually is quite different from the original. This same phenomenon is repeated over and over in organizations on a daily basis. Try it yourself. Tell someone a juicy bit of gossip about something that is about to happen in your organization but has not yet been announced. If you really want to ensure that this information hits the company grapevine, mention that because it hasn't been announced yet, it shouldn't be shared with anyone else. Now just sit back and wait until this rumor gets back to you. How long do you think it will take? In most organizations, the process probably won't take very long. Why? Because everyone just loves a rumor. People feel they are getting the inside scoop, and that's more fun than knowing about it from an official announcement. You probably never realized how much enjoyment you are taking away from people when you make official announcements and remove the information from the rumor mill!

The problem with the rumor mill is that people often make judgments based on the kind of highly speculative information it dispenses. For a variety of reasons, many employees would sooner believe a rumor heard at the water cooler than anything they hear from management. Important career decisions are sometimes based on rumors rather than on fact.

An active rumor mill is as much a function of management's ineffective approach to communication as it is of employees and their propensity for spreading rumors. Rumors fill the void created by lack of communication. Managers seriously underestimate the power of the need for communication. They are deceiving themselves if they think information won't leak out when something of importance is in the works.

The challenge for organizations is to utilize the powerful Natural Force of Communication in ways that prevent such adverse occurrences or at least minimize their negative impact. A good example of this Natural Force is the communication that takes place during any planned restructuring or reorganization. Regardless of management's efforts to keep sensitive information confidential until it is ready to share these developments with the rest of the workforce, the news inevitably leaks out. Rumor and speculation can run rampant throughout the organization.

Effective Leadership Requires Effective Communication

In the final analysis, leadership is all about communication. Think of the great leaders of the world, both past and present. Their ability to communicate effectively is perhaps their strongest commonality. Their messages continue to inspire and lead, even decades later. Winston Churchill, John F. Kennedy, Martin Luther King Jr., and Franklin D. Roosevelt, to name just a few, all had exceptional communication abilities that enabled them to change the world with their words, particularly in times of turmoil or crisis, when communication is most important.

It is during challenging times that the Communication Natural Force is at its strongest. You can either allow it to take over and control communication in your organization or you can exercise your leadership prerogative and control it yourself.

You don't have to be one of the greatest speakers in the world to achieve this goal of leading communication in your organization. No one expects you to be. What people do expect is that you try. Successful communication is, like anything else, mostly effort. If you are sincere in your communication and really try to be effective, people will recognize and appreciate your effort. They will forgive a great deal if they believe that you are being forthright with them. They look to you for guidance and wisdom every day but will depend on you more during times of crisis. They need you to provide some perspective on what is occurring in their increasingly complex and changing work world. You will ultimately be judged not so much on what you did to react to change but on how well you communicated your view of the future to everyone in the organization. The greatest leaders achieve this vision and are able to express it to others.

Six Levels of Organizational Communication

Six levels of communication can be found in most organizations today. These levels are presented below in a hierarchy ranging from the least effective to the most effective. It is important for managers to have an understanding of these levels so that they can really understand the power of the Communication Natural Force. Knowledge of these levels will increase managers' awareness of how their communication efforts affect the entire organization and give them a better idea of how they can move to a higher level.

Level 1: Negative Communication

As the name implies, negative communication can be less than zero. More than a simple absence of communication in an organization, it is the void created by the lack of communication when it is most urgently needed. Negative communication creates cavernous gaps in organizational knowledge that can seriously affect overall morale and ultimately productivity. Negative communication takes this Natural Force to new depths. When an organization declines to communicate during critical times, it allows this Natural Force to control all messages received by employees.

The organization might be in such a state of confusion that it is (at least momentarily) incapable of developing and sending any sort of communication to employees. There might be so much infighting among those in charge that they are unable to agree on what should be revealed to the general public or their employees. Or they may have mistakenly decided that the safest route is to say nothing. Neither of these outcomes will do anything but worsen the situation.

Just as a country looks to its leaders for guidance and words of wisdom during a crisis, so, too, do employees in an organization. Following the terrorist attacks on America on September 11, 2001, President George W. Bush was almost instantly transformed into a much more dynamic and decisive leader, enabling a shocked and grieving nation to cope with the terrible tragedies. Your employees need this same kind of effective leadership, particularly during stressful or difficult times or uncertainty. They expect their leadership to take command of this Natural Force and direct it in ways that provide them with guidance and understanding of the situation. When this doesn't happen, they are left with nothing but their own speculations and worries about what will come next. This Natural Force will overpower their imaginations, fueled by the all-powerful rumor mill, creating fears that are often larger than life.

There are still a few managers who subscribe to the "mushroom" theory of communication. They believe they can keep everyone in the dark and still expect them to develop. Although this philosophy may indeed work well with mushrooms, it isn't a good management practice to utilize when dealing with people.

Communication attempts that have an unintended adverse effect on those who receive the message also fall under this heading. One person's good news may be less than happily received by others. IBM portrayed such a situation in a television commercial in which the head of a young company announces to his employees that they have just landed a huge account. The ecstatic CEO is thinking about the growth this represents for the company and the financial rewards he will enjoy as a result of the new revenue coming in under his leadership. The employees, on the other hand, are thinking about the extra work and increased demands, and they groan rather than cheer on hearing his "good" news.

Level 2: Selected Communication

Selected communication is like using only the prettiest flowers to make a bouquet. This sanitized communication typically does not address any of the real substance of a situation and is designed to depict something in a certain light in the hope of influencing public opinion. This type of communication is usually sent to the media for public relations purposes, approved for release only after being filtered through the organization's top executives and legal department.

Selected communication is occasionally more complete and substantial but only on limited topics. For instance, many companies fall into the *bad news syndrome*. The bad news syndrome involves telling your employees all the bad economic news of the company but little of the good. Why would the leadership of a company want to do such a thing? It is often a matter of practicality. Divulging bad news about annual performance and profits tells employees not to expect big raises that year. Good economic news creates expectations of substantial raises. Managers caught in this syndrome find themselves more than happy to tell everyone how miserably the company performed, but they resist sharing good news about profitability and performance.

Level 3: Situational Communication

Situational communications are designed to fit certain occasions. For example, most formal organizational communications consist of highly scripted announcements that vary little from meeting to meeting. An organization might have an "economic crisis" communication that it dusts off when times get tough and "belt tightening" returns as the theme of the day.

In some situations, ceremonial-type messages are necessary and even expected, such as when a company announces new leadership or during a new leader's introductory visits to distant branches or subsidiaries of the organization. In these situations, communication between top levels of management and the workforce are probably at their best. The new leader might sit down and share a meal with those in operative positions in the organization and take time to listen to their hopes, concerns, and expectations. Unfortunately, this level of communication is often short-lived. Once the new leader is entrenched in his or her new role, there just never seems to be time to follow up with more situational communications, no matter how productive and well received they were before.

Level 4: Scheduled Communication

Scheduled communication is more a calendar function than an attempt to share information. These routine communications might be required by law or company policy and take place according to a predictable schedule each year. For example, the CEO's heartfelt holiday messages to employees might sound suspiciously similar from year to year. A company's annual shareholders' meeting and its annual report would also fall into this category. So would many of the meetings that are held throughout the year, such as monthly staff meetings, quarterly business updates, and budgeting meetings. Although they have the potential to be more, annual or semiannual performance evaluations are typically a form of scheduled communication and often take on the character of a chore rather than being a useful management development exercise.

Scheduled communications certainly have the potential to be a positive addition to an organization's overall communication efforts. Just because they are predictable doesn't necessarily mean they serve little purpose. To the contrary, their predictability can be their greatest strength. Employees might look forward to the arrival of these communications as long as they perceive them to be sincere.

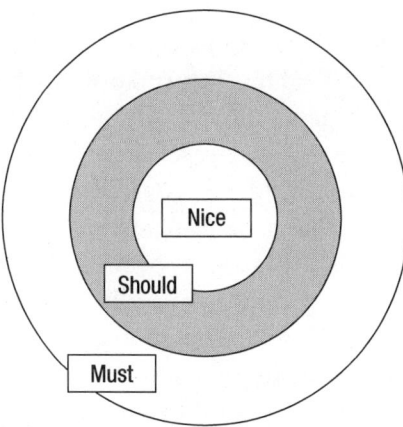

Figure 1 Communication Circles Model

Level 5: Candid Communication

Candid communication may be somewhat scarce in many organizations. It involves not only sharing the truth but doing so before the rumor mill is overflowing with news. Candid communications do not violate confidentiality agreements or reveal sensitive information that might have a damaging effect on the business if released too early. These examples of careless communications would obviously be very unproductive.

People don't really want to hear things that they are not supposed to hear. They will understand that certain information is protected, at least for the present, and will wait until the time is right to hear the news. However, they do object to not hearing the news when the time is right. The matter of timing is illustrated in Figure 1. The three circles can be described as follows:

Must: On the outer ring of this communication model are those communications that people *must* have in order to perform their jobs. There is no compromising this information. If employees don't get it, the job can't be done. Communication is nearly always at this basic and essential level.

Should: The next circle is information that employees *should* know. Note that the definition of *should* is different from the definition of *must*. We are not dealing with show-stopping information here. The employee can probably continue performing his or her job without this type of communication, albeit perhaps not as well. This information makes employees feel included in the organization's communication loop. There is probably nothing particularly sensitive about this information, nor is it likely to be considered confidential. It consists of details that give people a slight edge. It affords them a clearer understanding of the organization's overall direction and permits strategic thinking by giving them a glimpse of what others might be planning for the future. The absence of this type of communication inevitably results in statements such as "If I had only known that at the time, I would have...."

Nice: As its name implies, this information is simply nice to hear. It will probably have no impact on an individual's job, at least not in any direct sense. In fact, it may have nothing to do with the employee's job. This kind of communication is a courtesy, not a necessity. People greatly appreciate being included. This level of communication helps create better working relationships because sharing the information is an act of trust. Like everything else in life, you must give trust in order to receive it. Similarly, if you want to receive "nice to know" communication, you must extend it to others. Candid communication most often falls into this circle.

The difference between these three circles of communication is often a matter of timing. "Nice to know" communications are no longer at a premium after everyone else learns the news. Telling people "nice to know" information after the fact negates the objective of the exercise. "Nice to know" information can turn into "must know" in a very short period of time. How people will react and adapt to the information is often a function of when and how they hear it. It's fun to hear the news before everyone else does but frustrating to be the last to find out. When you communicate on a candid level by sharing "nice to know" information with your employees, you take away all the power of the rumor mill.

One type of communication is not shown on the circle but should be included in this discussion: information employees *shouldn't* know. As mentioned above, there is certain confidential information that should not be released. Employees will accept the response "I'm sorry but I can't answer that question because it involves confidential information" only if they feel it is sincere and they believe they are being told the truth. Their acceptance will also be greater if they are used to hearing "nice to know" information.

Level 6: Partnering Communication

Partners in an enterprise must share information consistently and equally with one another at all times. This level of communication is reciprocal and flows freely back and forth. Partners keep other partners aware of all information that is important to the enterprise's well-being and future. By withholding vital information, one partner may be jeopardizing the future for all. Even in a traditional organization, with its structure of various levels of management and responsibilities, there must be some sense of partnership. It might not seem like it, but at times management and workforce need to be on the same side and share the same goal—the success of the organization. Without success, there will be no jobs at all, at least not with that particular organization.

When communication reaches the partnering level in an organization, everyone is playing an active role in contributing to the shared goals and success of the organization. Partners typically want to share as much information as possible to help ensure that these goals are reached. They want not only to pass along information that might be useful to others but to receive the same type of useful information that will help them improve their job performance. They go to great lengths to ensure that as many employees as possible are participating at all three levels of the Communication Circles model.

New Rules of Communication

Any number of communications models have been developed over the years describing the interaction between a *sender* and a *receiver,* but they all have the same goal: to ensure that the intended message is the message that is received. The following rules will help you see the process through to a successful conclusion.

Take It Easy on Clichés

Clichés are actually a low form of communication. They might make you sound clever or in sync with the latest catchphrases going around business circles, but they can also make you a lazy communicator. Although they may serve as shortcuts to making a point by offering familiar analogies, they are often overused. Clichés have a legitimate place in conversation, but they can't replace the higher levels of communication. When people are seeking information, they don't want to hear clichés, which sound more like smoke screens than real communication. Using clichés in these circumstances is tantamount to conceding the communication battle to this Natural Force. Talk in real terms when communication is most important.

Make Contact

There is a big difference between talking *with* people and talking *at* people. Which do you do?

Talking at people is simply using your position and authority to get people's attention. The words are essentially meaningless. This type of communication is boring. Listeners can't wait for it to be over. In the meantime, they are either planning a way to get out of the situation or rehearsing their responses as they wait for an opportunity to get a word in edgewise.

Conversely, talking with people involves constant evaluation of their responsiveness and understanding, much of it based on non-verbal signs such as nodding in agreement, eye contact, or facial expression. Although these can be subtle, they are still very telling. They are windows into the listener's feelings and will tell you if you are making contact or not. Based on these signs, you can adjust your communication as necessary to make contact with the listener.

Be realistic about the effectiveness of your communication with others. Don't be deceived into thinking that you have communicated effectively when you have not. That will only make ineffective communication a bigger obstacle and increase the power of this Natural Force.

Communicate with Purpose

Prepare a communication plan. It doesn't have to be a massive media campaign designed to change public opinion (although it could); rather, it should be focused on the information you want others to receive from you. Be purposeful in your communication, even in casual conversation. This is not to say that everything you say should be carefully scripted or rehearsed, but there should be a purpose to every communication, even if it is simply to build relationships or enjoy someone's company. If you are not achieving your objective, end the communication. We waste too much time in unproductive communication. Either make your communication meet your objectives, or do something more productive.

Communicate Longer

When communication is productive or has the potential to be, stay with it. Get everything you can out of it. Realize that effective communication doesn't always occur and that it is a gift when it does. Work toward achieving this goal when the potential exists. Help others reach this objective when communicating with you. You may have to be patient and listen harder. Many people have much to say if they are only given the opportunity. Don't be so quick to dismiss a point or question as irrelevant. It may be like an iceberg, with its true mass below the surface. Find out what is really on people's minds and in their hearts. This is where you will find your most important communication with others.

Practice Communication Diplomacy

Communication is a lot like international diplomacy. There are certain expectations that must be honored. Although these expectations are mostly symbolic, they are extremely important. Violating these customs can set off incidents that have great political ramifications. The same is true of communication around sensitive issues. People often have certain hot buttons that you just shouldn't push unless you are purposely trying to upset them.

Certain issues or topics may best be avoided. Your method of approaching a topic is also important. Stating the other person's position on a subject to his or her satisfaction demonstrates that you have an accurate understanding of the other person's feelings and is an excellent way to begin this type of dialogue. Most important is to respect the other person's position and feelings on a sensitive subject. You will find this is usually the first step in achieving effective communication with that individual.

Communicate Fairly and Honestly

If you expect to have a continuing dialogue with others, you must communicate fairly and honestly with them at all times. Above all, you need to protect and ensure your credibility. When you have lost credibility, the Communication Natural Force will have its way. You will no longer be in control of any communication in your organization, even your own.

Credibility is like so many other important human characteristics. It usually takes a great deal of hard work to establish but can be lost in an instant. Fortunately, it can be regained. People have a keen eye and ear for credibility. They will give you another chance if they feel you are sincere and committed to honesty and fairness. Practice credibility, and you will be back in control of your own communications and better able to manage this Natural Force in your organization.

Show Up

With all the advances in communication technology, it is increasingly possible to be a long-distance manager. But ultimately, regardless of how sophisticated or widely available this technology becomes, there is no substitute for simply being there live and in person.

Organizations must be proactive in their communication programs, setting up systems that establish effective communications among all members. Some of these systems might involve new technology, such as the Internet, intranet, VMX, and videoconferencing. Others may be as basic as face-to-face meetings with managers and employees. We shouldn't ever think that face-to-face communication can be replaced with any type of technology. No matter how good teleconferencing technology becomes, it will always be less effective than actually being there—maybe more economical and practical but never as good. Be there whenever you can. Visit parts of your organization that you do not usually see. Let people know that you are a real person, not just a figurehead or a symbol. Talk face-to-face, shake hands, and break bread together. Your presence will always be the most effective form of communication.

Managing Communication

Organizations can utilize this Natural Force by bringing it into their planning early in the process, perhaps at the very beginning. Managers are constantly underestimating the power of the Communication Natural Force. They kid themselves about their ability to control it. They would be better off conceding the battle and moving with it rather than against it.

Adopt an Open Communication Approach

Organizations should focus on releasing information as early as possible instead of trying to find ways to keep it confidential for as long as they can. That way, they will at least be in control of what is being disclosed, and they can maintain their credibility. Remember, in a battle between you and a Natural Force, you should put your money on the force every time.

Think about the good that can come from implementing a different approach to communication in your organization. You won't be constantly fighting the losing battle of trying to keep confidential information confidential. As an experienced manager once said after being frustrated over and over again by leaks of sensitive information in his organization, "There is no such thing as confidentiality. As long as two people know something, regardless of their positions in the company, that information should no longer be considered confidential." Chasing rumors or denying the truth will only cause frustration for everyone. Instead, use the power of this Natural Force to try to get everyone's support for (or at least their commitment to) the coming changes. At the very least, you can establish greater credibility and trust with your employees by sharing information before the rumor mill begins to overflow with evidence that everybody's speculations are in fact the truth.

What is the downside of adopting a policy of open communication? What is really stopping you from communicating important information earlier? Managers often overestimate all the negative effects of releasing certain types of information. They may find that once the information does get out, either intentionally or unintentionally, the world doesn't stop turning. All the predictions of dire consequences and doom seldom come true. Instead, life goes on just as it did before.

The subject of salaries provides a good example. By regulation, the salaries of top executives in publicly held corporations must be disclosed annually, so this information is no big secret. Hourly employees' salaries are often contained in a collective bargaining agreement or are posted openly in the organization each year. But salary information of mid-level managers has typically been a closely guarded secret. These employees are trying very hard to rise in the organization. They inhabit a highly competitive work environment in which their career fates can be determined by many factors, not the least of which is the performance of other middle managers who aspire to the same jobs. Salaries at this level typically are based on performance, and the content of an individual's performance evaluation is usually something that is known only by the employee and his or her supervisor. In its most effective form, a performance evaluation is a personalized assessment of a person's strengths and weaknesses. Performance evaluations are usually tied closely to raises and ultimately will determine the individual's salary. All this potentially sensitive and personal information is not something you would want posted on a bulletin board.

Companies generally have an unwritten rule prohibiting management employees at this level from discussing salary information with one another. However, this practice is beginning to change with the times. The Clinton administration focused heavily on pay equity issues, particularly as related to women. Published reports indicated that women's salaries were lagging behind those of their male counterparts (see chapter 5). Recent legislation and regulatory guidelines have focused on bridging these gaps, with the result that the courts are less understanding and permissive of unofficial or even official rules of salary confidentiality when pay discrimination cases are brought before them. Many contend that these practices may indeed contribute to gender-based pay differences. The old adage "What you don't know can't hurt you" might come to mind. In other words, if you don't know that you are making less than someone who is similarly situated except for gender or race, you won't complain about the pay discrepancy. If this is truly the intent of these confidentiality practices, the issue may be debated in the courts for many years to come.

But the practice of keeping mum on salaries has changed, perhaps forever. Organizational norms discouraging discussion of salaries will likely be replaced by full and open disclosure. Holding on to practices and rules that forbid these kinds of discussions likely will also become a thing of the past. Doing so will only force you to fight an uphill battle against the Communication Natural Force.

Think Strategically About Communication

Organizations that have learned to think strategically about their communication efforts begin planning what they want to say on certain topics well in advance. If business was poor during the past fiscal year, they may begin sending out messages about their lower performance in an effort to dampen expectations. Targeted groups might be the hourly workforce, union leadership, executives whose salaries are largely incentive and bonus based, and even the company's shareholders, who may have to be prepared for lower dividends or stock values.

One problem with this type of strategic communication is that messages occasionally get mixed. A message meant to serve one purpose bleeds over to another targeted group for which it was not designed or intended. For example, an organization might want to inform the workforce that it is once again belt-tightening time and employees should not expect big wage increases during upcoming contract negotiations. We see this type of communication in newsletters sent out by many automobile or airline corporations to their unions' leadership and members. They also may be hoping to influence public and political opinion with these strategic communications. If the general public can be convinced not to support a strike by a major union, this can put a lot of pressure on the union to agree to the company's proposals. Politicians may also be reluctant to support a special interest group's fight for higher wages and benefits if it means that voters are negatively affected by a prolonged strike. This pressure is felt keenly every time an airline is grounded by a major strike, often causing even the president of the United States to get into the act. The company's stockholders are also hearing the message. Wall Street does not look favorably on impending labor problems and often reacts negatively to such news in terms of the company's stock price.

The reverse situation could also exist when a company attempts to persuade stockholders to look favorably on it as an investment. The organization may publicize its record last-quarter or year-end earnings, yet despite the company's notable performance, it may still be premature to start popping champagne corks in celebration. Maybe there was a nonrecurring reason for these positive numbers, or perhaps the results were a function of accounting procedures rather than of performance. The company is now between the proverbial rock and a hard place. It wants to use the good news to attract shareholders, but, at the same time, it doesn't want to increase labor costs by creating expectations for future wage and benefit improvements. The lesson here is that in order to better manage this Natural Force, you must consider a number of factors affecting your communication efforts, including your intended audience and the unintended messages you may be sending to others who will also hear this information.

Use Technology to Enable Communication

Advances in technology have opened many avenues of communication of which we never even dreamed just a few years ago. Developments such as the Internet, intranets, electronic mail, voice mail, teleconferences, faxes, cell phones, pagers, and microcomputers have both changed and challenged the potential of this Natural Force. All this new technology does cost money, but the price of talk today is relatively inexpensive, particularly compared to its potential payoffs. In most organizations, these new technologies have become a core requirement of doing business in the electronic age. The real challenge is to utilize this technology to move in the direction of the Communication Natural Force.

Although the connection between computers and Natural Forces may become blurred in the midst of all the technology that goes into the introduction of each new operating system, a definite relationship does exist. Just as earlier inventions such as the printing press and telephone enabled this Natural Force to move forward in powerfully decisive ways, so, too, will today's electronic breakthroughs, although probably at a much faster speed. This Natural Force isn't really about the technology itself but about what it can enable. You can either help by becoming a *communication enabler* or you can be rolled over by this Natural Force. Presented in this way, it appears to be a simple choice. Unfortunately for many managers, even today, it is not.

Not only can anyone say anything, but with today's technology, those words can be transmitted to everyone in the organization in a microsecond. This can be both a blessing and a curse. These new tools will make a good communicator even more effective, but a poor communicator will find that they magnify this weakness by many powers. The Communication Natural Force will reveal this deficiency like an open microphone catching messages that were never intended for broadcast. The biggest problem is that people often don't realize they need help to become better communicators.

For example, a vice president who headed a division of a large retail corporation in the 1980s decided he wanted to be like his hero, Lee Iacocca, who at that time was leading Chrysler's revitalization by acting as the company's advertising pitchman and media icon. Unfortunately, this vice president lacked the on-camera sincerity and credibility that enabled Iacocca to convince Americans that the truly patriotic thing to do was to buy American cars, particularly Chryslers, instead of foreign imports.

The vice president began a series of videotaped communications intended to inspire the workforce. The result fell far short of his goal. He came across as arrogant and condescending rather than inspirational. These same personality characteristics also prevented him from getting any real feedback about his on-screen (as well as off-screen) image from his underlings in the organization. Caught in an "emperor's new clothes" syndrome, nobody had the nerve to tell him that the store managers who received these videos with strict instructions to show them to all their employees really dreaded the tapes' arrival. The videos created an employee relations nightmare almost every time they were shown.

Today's challenge is not really communication transmittal, as it used to be, but effective use of these new tools in order to manage this Natural Force. However, in the midst of all this technology, the same basic rules still apply. Understanding and being reminded of these rules can serve you well through each new phase of technology to come.

The following chart is a quick reference for the Communication Natural Force. It provides examples of ways to better manage or influence this force, specific actions or programs you might implement, and the impact these actions could have on employees.

Quick Reference for the Communication Natural Force		
INFLUENCE ON NATURAL FORCE	MANAGEMENT ACTIONS	IMPACT ON EMPLOYEES
Business updates	Keep the workforce informed through regularly scheduled meetings or printed materials.	Increases understanding of what is going on in the business and how it might affect their jobs.
Performance feedback	Institute and monitor formal performance-feedback systems.	Provides personalized and specific feedback on job performance and evaluation by a supervisor.
Business strategy	Share short- and long-term business strategies with employees.	Creates increased support for the plan.
Financial information	Consistently share information about the organization's financial performance.	Increases understanding of the organization's financial performance.
Sales and marketing reports	Let everyone know about marketplace response to the organization's products and/or services.	Enables employees to address any customer problems and continue to do what is best received in the marketplace.
Business applications	Educate employees about the practical business applications of new actions or processes.	Increases understanding of the reasons for certain actions or decisions concerning these applications.
Budgets and cost controls	Share budgets and cost reports with employees on all levels.	Empowers employees to manage budgets and make more responsible decisions concerning expenditures.
Benefits administration	Make sure employees have a good understanding of how to utilize their benefits most effectively.	Creates well-educated consumers of health services who also have a better appreciation of their benefits.
Board of directors reports	Publish or share information on the board's actions and decisions.	Offers a glimpse into the types of decisions and issues that are part of their board's responsibilities.
CEO messages	Establish a number of ways to get the message out to employees.	Increases understanding of the direction in which the CEO is planning to lead the organization.
Newsletter	Publish regularly so employees learn to depend on it as a source of important organizational information.	Provides a familiar, internal printed-media source for information and reference.

Mission

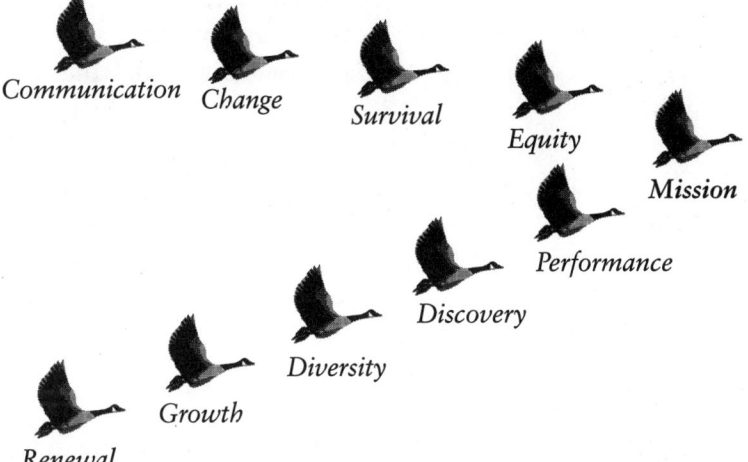

Communication Change Survival Equity Mission

Performance

Discovery

Diversity

Growth

Renewal

LAWS OF THE MISSION NATURAL FORCE

- A mission provides guidance for an organization.

- An effective mission is understood by everyone.

- Vision and mission go hand in hand.

- Missions have their price.

A mission is important to an organization as a source of direc tion. Without a clear mission to let its members know where they are headed, the organization can seem like a ship lost at sea, drifting aimlessly.

A Mission Provides Guidance for an Organization

We all need guidance in our lives. We need something to give us direction, something stable, solid, and unfaltering that we can depend on at all times. Just as ships in the night need lighthouse beacons to direct their journeys and warn of dangerous passages, organizations require this same type of guidance. Dr. Stephen Covey (1989), in his best-selling book *The 7 Habits of Highly Effective People,* likens a lighthouse to a principle, something that doesn't change. Dr. Covey tells the story of a ship's captain who, while guiding his mighty vessel in the middle of the night, sighted a light in the distance and thought it was another ship. The captain transmitted a message ordering this obstacle to make way, only to be informed that he was actually trying to tell a lighthouse to change its location. An organization's mission will serve as a beacon of light if it is developed and utilized properly. A mission can be a powerful force when it reaches its true and full potential.

An Effective Mission Is Understood by Everyone

There once was a ship's captain who, for reasons known only to him, set out to sea without ever telling any of his crew where they were headed. He steered his ship far out into the ocean on a definite course that was a secret even to those who helped operate the vessel. The crew, by virtue of their nautical experience, had a vague idea of where they were traveling on this mysterious journey, but without knowledge of their destination, they were uncertain of their exact location at any time. Unfortunately, the captain died in his sleep one night, and the crew found themselves in the middle of the ocean, not knowing where they were, how they had gotten there, or what course they should follow to return to port. Total confusion and chaos ensued as they argued among themselves as to their course of action. Without leadership or a mission, they drifted aimlessly for weeks, eventually perishing.

Missions are not "need to know" information; they should be communicated to everyone on board. Employees can't truly support something they haven't been told about or don't understand. You never know when they may be called on to help "steer the ship" in these rapidly changing business times and circumstances. Without guidance, they will search for their own mission, looking beyond the organization to sources such as labor unions, outside agencies, the legal system, and competitors. Without a clear mission, this Natural Force begins to pull the organization apart, because there is no unifying message that gives everyone in the organization a common focus.

This is why some organizations operate most effectively and efficiently during times of crisis. The crisis itself gives everyone a common purpose and objective. All employees understand what the end result is supposed to be and receive clear direction from leaders on how to reach this goal. Communications are usually significantly better than they are under normal circumstances, and frequent updates and progress reports are provided to everyone. Once the crisis has been resolved, the results of this overall team effort are shared, and both individual and group efforts are adequately recognized.

Unfortunately, after the crisis has passed, the organization may go back to its normal mode of operation and retain few of the positive characteristics that contributed to its survival. Employees no longer have a clear and unifying mission. Communications and recognition go back to being random or absent. There is less sense of teamwork, and individualism takes over once again, with people seemingly at work on their own little islands, isolated from the rest. The organization's leaders begin to wonder why everyone worked together so well in a crisis but can't seem to get much accomplished on an everyday basis. In some ways, they may even miss the crisis because people worked together so well as they tried to resolve the problem. Being part of an effective team is an exhilarating experience, with each member's contributions valued and appreciated by the rest. There is nothing more satisfying for a leader of a group or team than to see everyone working together successfully to achieve a common goal.

An organization's mission should provide employees with direction and goals. Employees today expect, even demand, that their leaders define a clear mission that will guide them as they perform their jobs. When a well-conceived mission is freely communicated and shared, it can be a powerful force that inspires employees with a sense of purpose.

Vision and Mission Go Hand in Hand

An organization's mission is not really practical if it doesn't provide the vision needed to be successful in the future. Vision without mission is like a great idea that never gets implemented. It's difficult to say which should come first, but the point is that you can't have one without the other. Some leaders are more adept at developing the organization's mission and explaining its purpose and why it exists, while others are better at envisioning the organization's future. To really be able to harness the power of this Natural Force, you need both vision and mission. Vision tells you where you need to be in the future; mission tells you how to get there.

Of these two leadership skills, vision may be the harder to teach. Developing a mission is similar to other tasks that a manager must master in order to be successful. A mission is really nothing more than a strategic plan for the organization's future boiled down to a paragraph or two. Certainly this is no easy task, but learning to become a visionary is another challenge entirely. It is different from any other managerial skill taught in MBA programs or acquired through experience.

The power of vision cannot be underestimated. Without vision, none of the world's great discoveries or inventions would have come into existence. Someone had to envision what life would be like as a result of these discoveries and inventions. It was this vision that drove our forebears to seek out better ways in which to live.

Yet vision alone doesn't ensure success. You have to make the vision work. Think of how many times Thomas Edison tried to invent the lightbulb or the struggles Apple Computer has undergone. It has been said that everything looks like a failure at the midpoint. Truly great visionaries are not easily discouraged. They persevere despite the obstacles and setbacks they encounter as they try to achieve their vision. They push on even when their staunchest supporters have long since abandoned the cause. It is the power of their vision, more than any other factor, that makes the next great discovery possible.

Missions Have Their Price

Times of transition or crisis are the real tests of an organization's commitment to its stated mission. This is when "window dressing" missions begin to unravel, for it is at moments when value decisions must be made that the real heart and soul of the organization are revealed.

You can learn a lot about an organization by watching the way it handles crises. It is relatively easy to be noble during good times, but bad times present different challenges. Every organizational system is tested in one way or another. Leaders show just how serious they are about their convictions. Many other Natural Forces begin to pull on the organization, like passengers on a sinking ship fighting for a place in one of the few available lifeboats.

Everyone will be able to see if the organization can walk like it talks. If an oil company says it is committed to protecting the environment, the public expects it to react in certain ways when a fuel spill from a huge ocean tanker threatens a sensitive area. If an automobile company brags about passenger protection and then discovers a safety design problem in its vehicles, people expect to see recalls or repairs regardless of the expense and its effect on quarterly profit margins. On a subtler level, if a company claims that service is its number one priority but fails to meet customer requirements, it is expected to remedy the situation even at the risk of inconvenience or financial loss.

Nobility has its price. To profess to have a noble purpose is one thing, but to pay substantially to stand by those words can be a different matter entirely. This is when the rubber meets the road and you hope the tire doesn't fall apart. That is exactly what happened with Firestone's tires, particularly those on Ford Explorers, and the company had to make huge decisions about how to deal with this situation from both an ethical and a legal standpoint. The results will affect the company's future for many years to come.

Types of Organizational Missions

There are a number of different types of organizational missions, not all of which serve the same purpose. These types are *Public Relations Missions, Reality Missions,* and *Working Missions.*

Public Relations Missions

Public Relations Missions, or PR Missions, are the most common of the three types of missions. PR Missions can be achieved, but you must be realistic about where you stand on the journey. These missions usually reflect the way the organization wants to be perceived rather than its current reality. Their greatest utility, as the name implies, is as public relations tools, and they can function as employee relations tools as well. PR Mission statements are usually displayed in the lobbies of businesses or included in advertisements to try to create a certain public image for the organization. PR Mission statements say things like "providing the highest-quality customer service is our number one priority." Many companies have tried, sometimes even successfully, to change their public images with similar mission statements directed at consumers. In theory at least, this statement serves as an inspiration to the organization's employees, encouraging them to strive to reach this level and let the world know about their commitment to quality and service.

However, regardless of whether or not these objectives are achieved, the PR Mission statement lives on. The problem is that it continues to exist even when it is not legitimate. To be honest, some of these missions might be better named "Mission Impossible," and in these cases, mission statements serve only as window dressing in the reception areas of businesses or as nicely framed pictures in conference rooms.

Reality Missions

There is obviously a reason why every organization exists, some underlying strategy for surviving at any given time in an organization's existence, although it might not always be quantified or communicated. This represents the Reality Mission of the organization. A Reality Mission is not something you would put on the wall of your lobby or include in your advertising. Instead, you use a Reality Mission to check your current position in terms of your overall business strategy and goals.

Reality Missions probably do not reflect leadership's aspirations for the organization but address the situation as it actually is, so when the organization's leaders confuse the way they want things to be and the way things really are, they are headed for some problems.

It is dangerous to lose track of the distinction between goals and reality. Thinking you're better off than you are makes for a bad situation. You could find yourself in the same position as that ship's crew, arguing about where you are and how to get back home. For example, a Reality Mission might sound something like this: "The current Reality Mission of our organization is to keep costs down enough to show a modest profit during the next quarter; this will keep the shareholders and everyone off our backs for the rest of the fiscal year." Granted, it's not the most lofty of mission statements, but it may be the truth. This organization should be asking itself if it is satisfied with its current Reality Mission. In some cases, the most important thing to do is to take a long hard look at where you are and where you are going. Think about what your Reality Mission might sound like if you wrote it honestly to reflect your current situation. What would your true Reality Mission be?

Working Missions

Working Missions are the most useful of the three because they are the most practical. The success or utility of a mission statement may depend largely on whom it is written for or whom it is designed to influence. Mission statements can be useful to employees working toward a shared goal if the statement truly gives them direction and understanding of purpose.

For a good example of a Working Mission, let's consider the situation of a small warehouse in the Midwest, where a team of employees was struggling to define its goals for a particular task that had been assigned by the facility manager. The manager was concerned about the rising costs of the packaging materials needed to ensure that the company's product reached customers without breakage, and she wisely decided that this mission must be clearly understood by all involved before they undertook the project. Employees and manager spent days trying to describe their mission. They wrote one grandiose PR Mission statement after another, overstating what they could realistically accomplish. Each statement was systematically challenged by one of the team members and was then dismissed. Finally a team member said in frustration, "Aren't we just trying to reduce packaging costs? Then why don't we just say that?" Everyone was astonished by the simplicity and accuracy of this statement. "To reduce packaging costs" became the team's Working Mission statement. It provided guidance as team members constantly checked their procedures against the stated objective. If they realized that certain proposed actions or changes didn't support the mission, they didn't implement them. Obviously, a mission statement does not have to be long or complex in order to reflect an effective Working Mission. In most cases, the simpler the mission, the better.

Effective Mission Statements

Effective mission statements send the same message to both clients and employees while also providing useful and practical guidance to the organization.

Include All Three Types

Ideally, a mission should serve all three of the above purposes: it should tell the world what the organization represents, describe the current situation in the organization, and serve as a practical tool for everyone working in the organization. Is it possible to have such a mission? Yes, it is. It may take considerable thought and effort, but the hard work will be worth it in the end.

Too many organizations develop mission statements that meet one of the criteria but not the others. Typically, missions are focused on public relations. Leaders can't understand why employees aren't embracing this mission and making it part of their everyday motivation. The reason should now be obvious. The mission probably didn't address the reality of the organization or the way it currently operates. More than anything, a mission must be credible. If it is not, it will quickly be dismissed as nothing more than a publicity stunt, not worth the fancy picture frame in which it is mounted.

Many organizations around the world have developed very effective mission statements that serve all three objectives. One example is the mission statement of the Bizet Group of Pittsburgh, a worldwide career center that provides placement, retention, training and development, and outplacement services. The group's mission reads as follows:

- Do great work
- Make a buck
- Have fun

In these eight words, group members have described their commitment to meeting the needs of the customer, the organization, and its employees. All three objectives can be met and are not mutually exclusive. In fact, each objective should support and enhance the likelihood of the other two. They depend on one another.

Vehicle for Achieving the Most Critical Goals

The mission should not become the overall purpose itself. In other words, it should be a vehicle for achieving the most critical goals of the organization, not just the objective. It must be more than merely a values statement. Efforts at trying to reach a shared mission may be misdirected if the overall objective is not clearly understood. The wrong behaviors and even values could be justified in the name of the mission.

An organization may state an objective without understanding why it is being pursued in the first place. For example, one company was struggling to write a mission statement that would be accepted by its workers. It had recently implemented a teamwork concept and was in the process of changing many of the duties and responsibilities of employees at all levels. As part of this process, the head of the company's human resources department was leading a team of employees who were trying to craft a mission statement. They came up with the following: "Our company's mission is to become a team-based organization, enabling decision making and problem solving to take place at the lowest possible levels."

The team members presented their statement to the president of the company for approval so they could move forward and publicize the new mission. Everyone thought he would be delighted with the focus on the teamwork concepts he himself had introduced and supported so enthusiastically. But the same president of the company who had the vision to encourage team concepts in the organization was curiously dissatisfied with the mission statement. He kept reading it over and over without fully understanding what was bothering him so much. Finally, it dawned on him. Creating a team-based work culture was a means to an end, not the mission itself. Simply put, the mission of the company was to serve its customers, make a profit, and, it was to be hoped, somehow enrich the lives of its employees and their families.

The team's mission statement was the equivalent of leaving up the ladders and scaffolding after completing the construction of a building. All you really want in the end is the completed project. You don't have to show everyone how it was constructed. The same is true when it comes to writing mission statements. You don't have to tell them how you plan to get there, just where you are heading. Don't leave your road maps lying all around in your mission statement. Fold them up nicely and put them back in the glove box for the next time you may need them to guide you along your way.

Twelve Steps to Becoming a Visionary

How can you become a visionary? It would help if you were clairvoyant and able to see into the future. Assuming that you are not, the following tips may help you become a visionary in your organization. As you can see, none of these suggestions requires supernatural powers; instead, they involve paying attention to things that are happening around you.

Step 1: Be a Possibility Thinker

A possibility thinker is someone who looks at the possibilities rather than the impossibilities. These thinkers are constantly optimistic. The best salespeople are possibility thinkers; they believe that it is possible to sell anything to anyone. It is often this attitude that creates opportunities and, ultimately, sales. The same outlook can help you become a better visionary.

Step 2: Listen to Your Intuition

Visionaries listen to their gut feelings, although this doesn't mean they act capriciously. They believe in the power of their intuition and seek ways to validate their senses and feelings.

Step 3: Act on Your Ideas
Visionaries turn thoughts into actions. There are many people who have lots of great ideas but never do anything to make them a reality. Visionaries don't just see the future; they make it happen as well.

Step 4: Ignore the Skeptics
Unfortunately, there are many more skeptics than visionaries in this world. If you are a visionary, you will encounter many who will tell you that your ideas are foolhardy and should be abandoned. During Chrysler's revival, CEO Lee Iacocca used to say in one of his television commercials, "You either need to lead, follow, or get out of the way." This would be good advice for your skeptics. They should come up with a better idea, follow your vision, or keep quiet and stop trying to stand in the way of your vision.

Step 5: Dream Big
It's your dream, so you might as well make it as big as you want it to be. There is no sense in having small dreams. If you are going to dream a better tomorrow, why not make it the best vision possible? Imagine what would have happened if Walt Disney had dreamed of building a small amusement park when he first envisioned Disneyland. The result would have been entirely different, and people of all ages would be denied the distinctly magical experience of visiting Disney theme parks around the world. While you are at it, dream in Technicolor. Make your dreams as vibrant and exciting as possible. They may end up being more like black and white, but at least you will start off with a colorful vision. No matter what, you may be able to add a few colors along the way as your dream begins to become reality.

Step 6: Accept the Risks
Every vision has inherent risks. You need to accept these risks and consequences as part of the game. Every great visionary in history has had to pay the price for his or her dreams. If you can't accept the consequences, you may never be able to achieve your vision. You must be prepared for a few setbacks along the way.

Step 7: Failure Does Not Mean Your Vision Is Wrong
Great visionaries not only persevere despite continuing failures and frustrations; they also are not easily convinced that their vision is

wrong despite all the evidence that supports this conclusion. They believe in their visions and will protect them as if they were their children. They will do everything they can to nurture these children and help them develop. For visionaries, their missions often become their life's work. Setbacks and failures only tell them that they must try harder to turn their visions into reality.

It is vital that you fight for your mission if you truly believe in its importance. If you do not, others may dismiss it as a good idea that wasn't practical to implement. Remember, if it was easy to accomplish, it probably would already have been done.

Step 8: Be Willing to Compromise

Life is filled with compromises, and we don't always or even usually get exactly what we want. There are times when we have to accept compromises. Compromise and failure are two different things. Unfortunately, people often confuse these two concepts. Compromising some aspect of your vision in order to bring it to fruition doesn't mean you have failed; it means that you were insightful and wise enough to realize that your vision would not be possible at all without at least some compromise. You need to be flexible whenever it is appropriate and necessary for achieving your mission.

Step 9: Visions Don't Have End Points

Visions don't end but live on in different forms and formats in the future. Be prepared to live with your visions, because they don't always go away quickly or easily. Visions become a force of their own. As more people believe in them, they become more powerful. The work of the great visionaries of the world continues to exist even after they are gone. Visions are eternal. Just as the words "I have a dream," spoken by civil rights leader Martin Luther King Jr., continue to inspire and guide people many years after his death, dreams can live on.

Step 10: Get Others to See Your Vision

This isn't always easy to accomplish. It can be difficult to get others to share and appreciate your vision at first, but once they do, they, too, could become believers. You may need to work as hard at accomplishing this step as you do at making your vision a reality.

This is often the most important part of the entire process, for without the support of others, you will not be able to achieve your vision. Don't assume that everyone will accept the vision once it is achieved if they didn't do so in the beginning. Secure as much early support as you can, even if you must delay moving forward until you do. As with most great challenges, communication (see chapter 3) will be paramount.

Step 11: Drive Your Vision

Every cause or idea needs a sponsor. Without a sponsor as the driving force, even great ideas often run out of gas. You must expect to drive your vision over the bumps and through the turns it will inevitably encounter on its way to becoming reality. It's probably not realistic to expect others to jump into the driver's seat and begin steering your vision to its final destination. You may be the only one who truly knows the direction the vision needs to take, so settle into the driver's seat, put your vision in gear, and start moving forward.

Step 12: Forgive the Naysayers

For many, there is a lot of truth in the saying "I'm just a born skeptic." It's human nature to be skeptical. These people will likely meet the introduction of anything new with great resistance and reservation. They will also be the first to say "I knew this was a great idea all along" when it looks like your vision is going to be a great success. Be forgiving of these folks, for they can't really help themselves. Accept their newfound support as if they had offered it all along. You will need their help to keep the vision moving forward. Later is better than never. When people change their minds, it is a testament to the power of the vision, because it has converted skeptics into supporters.

Managing the Mission

Everyone has a need to understand what the organization stands for and why it exists. This is particularly true for new and prospective employees. They need to know if the organization's values are compatible with theirs, how well they will fit into the organization, and if there are mutually agreeable goals that they and the organization can achieve together. Most employee turnover is based to some degree on incompatibility between the organization's mission and the needs and goals of the individual employee. The problem is that these differences are often more perceptual in nature than real. Poor communication of the mission, not incompatibility of goals, may be the reason for turnover. When more than one Natural Force comes into play, managing the situation becomes an even greater challenge.

If your organization already has a mission statement, you may want to review it to make sure that it still expresses the organization's original meaning and purpose or is understood accurately. If you don't have a mission, develop one, accepting as much input as possible from as many people as possible. Don't be satisfied with just a few words that would make a nicely framed picture in your lobby; instead, create something that will have real meaning for your employees. This may not be a simple 30-minute exercise but may require considerable energy and effort. Take your mission seriously, or others never will.

Ensure an Effective and Meaningful Mission

Today's mission will guide your organization into the future, so it had better be a good one. Will your mission have a positive or negative influence on your organization's future? Of course, only time will tell, but you can do a few things today to help ensure that you have an effective and meaningful mission.

- Don't try to predict the future with your mission. It is not a crystal ball or a fortune-teller's tea leaves. It is a statement about your organization's justification for existence and future direction.

- Don't carve it in stone. Missions must be dynamic and designed to adapt to changing times.

- Don't expect everyone to be able to recite your mission verbatim on command. This will just embarrass people and perhaps even you. Settle for a general understanding of what the mission represents.

- Don't try to make your mission more than it is. Keep it simple. It shouldn't try to solve all of the world's problems, just a few that are important to your organization.

Find a Mission

It can be an interesting and challenging exercise to develop your own personal mission statement, especially if you have never done it before. All the principles discussed in this chapter are applicable to your personal mission. You will find this a revealing experience. Review your mission from time to time to see if you are making progress toward achieving it or if it should be redefined. Just as the needs of organizations change, yours will, too. Different times give rise to different goals. Set your own course and follow your dreams.

Perhaps one of the greatest contributions you can make in this world is to help someone else find direction and satisfaction. You can be a powerful force for others, not only those who report to you at work but people in your personal life as well. As Dag Hammarskjöld, former secretary-general of the United Nations, once said, "It is more noble to give yourself completely to one individual than to labor diligently for the salvation of the masses." A mission is more effective when it is focused on a realistic goal rather than on one that has been exaggerated beyond practicality. Don't underestimate the value of helping even one individual. You may not save the world, but, like Walt Disney, you can make it a better place in which to live.

A mission can be the most powerful force in your life if you take it seriously. It can lead and direct you to better destinations. Without a clear mission to pursue, you are like the crew of the ship lost at sea without their captain. Find your own mission first and then help others find theirs, both collectively and as individuals. You will find that the winds of this Natural Force will fill your sails as you continue your life's journey.

The following chart is a quick reference for the Mission Natural Force. It provides examples of ways in which to better manage or influence this force, specific actions or programs you might implement, and the impact these actions could have on employees.

Quick Reference for the Mission Natural Force

INFLUENCE ON NATURAL FORCE	MANAGEMENT ACTIONS	IMPACT ON EMPLOYEES
Recruitment literature	Project a certain image of the organization to the world.	Distinguishes fact from fiction when it comes to these printed materials.
New employee orientations	Attempt to instill its preferred perceptions of the company in new employees.	New employees might believe the initial message, but it must stand up to what they eventually learn about the organization.
Shareholder communications	Design communications to create positive images among shareholders and favorably influence their investment decisions.	Delivers a mixed message.
Reception area display	Usually fill the area with company propaganda.	Attracts little attention and is dismissed as nothing more than PR.
Business strategy	Specify the business plan for the organization.	Increases understanding of where the organization is headed.
Employee meetings	Regularly gather together employees from various levels to hear plans for the future.	Fosters belief only if they are sincere and communicate honestly.
Mission statements	Try to ensure a positive impact on the organization and the outside world.	Provides direction and guidance, but only if mission statements are credible.

Equity

Mission Communication Change Survival Equity Performance Discovery Diversity Growth Renewal

LAWS OF THE EQUITY
NATURAL FORCE

- People expect democracy in an organization.

- Equity is a balancing act.

- Inequity has a point of no return.

- Inequity evokes powerful emotions.

- Equity is in the eye of the beholder.

Equity is about fairness, either perceived or real. For employees in an organization, perception is reality when it comes to fairness. People are very concerned about how fairly they believe they are being treated. This Natural Force can stir up much emotion and influence employees' behaviors and attitudes toward the organization.

People Expect Democracy in an Organization

Democracy is the expected organizational system. Even though the structure in most organizations is not based specifically on democratic principles, equity is still a strong influence, particularly in companies that are based in the United States. Employees at all levels are concerned about getting their fair share of the corporate pie. Equity issues also involve administration of policies and practices. Employees are understandably concerned about whether they are being treated equally and fairly.

Equity Is a Balancing Act

Equity is achieved in an organization when both labor and management feel that they are being treated equally and fairly. As evidenced by what has happened in the steel industry over the past 100 or more years, when this balance tips too far in either direction, the entire system is jeopardized. If workers negotiate wages and benefits that make the company uncompetitive, the company will lose out to its competitors, but if the company doesn't share the rewards of its success with its workers, its behavior may create labor problems such as strikes and employee turnover. In addition, if the company becomes too successful, the government might step in and break it up into smaller parts, as happened with AT&T. The wise manager becomes concerned when inequity develops in either direction.

Inequity Has a Point of No Return

When there is perceived unfairness, the Natural Force of Equity begins to take over. It manifests itself in labor conflicts or strikes, employee turnover, government intervention, legal action and lawsuits, and even sabotage or workplace violence. The time to take action is before the situation reaches the point of no return. Once wages get out of control, it is hard to ask for concessions, and after employees lose faith that management will treat them fairly, it is difficult for them to regain that trust.

Inequity Evokes Powerful Emotions

People talk to one another about the inequities, both perceived and real, they have suffered on the job. They feed off one another's emotions. Tremendous energy is stored and released in these emotions, which can be overpowering for people who are not prepared to deal with them. This Natural Force can lead to decisions that might never be made otherwise. People often rationalize their irrational behavior by saying they were acting to correct an inequity or injustice in their lives.

Equity Is in the Eye of the Beholder

To the worker, it may appear that equity is something the company rations out only when it feels like it and when doing so is to its benefit. The company may feel that it can't get employees to listen seriously even when the message is critically important.

For example, in the late 1970s when the U.S. steel industry began to crumble due to cheaper imported products, the big steel makers went to the unions and warned them of impending doom. The companies asked the steelworkers for concessions that might help save them from plant closings, which were certain to occur without such agreements. Despite the high salaries that they had negotiated over the years, union members were skeptical about giving anything back to the company. They thought the companies' requests were just another scare tactic that would line corporate pockets with more profits from their sweat and hard work. Even today, this skepticism exists. Those steel industry giants of yesterday that managed to survive, such as LTV, U.S. Steel, and Bethlehem Steel, still face the same standoff with the Steelworkers Union over the identical issue of equity, even as survival is still very much in the balance for these companies today.

The problem is that truth truly is a point of view. Compelling arguments can almost always be made for either side. Despite the megadollar rulings against them, big companies like Coca-Cola argue very convincingly that they are committed to equal opportunity and advancement of minorities in their organizations. They can cite countless examples of minority employees attaining higher positions as a result of their affirmative action programs and initiatives. Microsoft will argue that it has merely been highly successful at providing quality products and customer service in the most efficient and cost-effective manner possible. Why should the company be penalized for achieving the same goal that every one of its competitors is also striving to reach? Like beauty, equity is often in the eye of the beholder.

Managing Equity

It is critical to reach a balance between organizational effectiveness and equity. Managers should understand and appreciate this innate need for equity on the part of employees at all levels of the organization. As a manager, you may not always be able to do much about these inequities, but you should at least understand how others feel about the issues. Business and market necessities must be considered and communicated to your employees. Unless the issue of equity is addressed or, at a minimum, acknowledged, organizations will constantly be charged with (perceived or real) unfairness. Your employees want you to make the right decisions even if your choices are unpopular. Ultimately, they would rather experience some inequities at work than face unemployment. They will accept the business case and rationalizations for inequities if they are aware of the situation and understand why these inequities are necessary. However, the pendulum will swing decisively in the other direction if they believe the organization is taking advantage of them.

It is particularly important to be aware of and sensitive to equity issues when you are considering major policy changes or introducing new personnel systems. Although equity and fairness may be a point of view more than anything else, it is always wise to consider as many perspectives as possible. Employee committees, ad hoc teams, and surveys are all excellent ways of addressing the Equity Natural Force. Talk to your groups, pay attention to their input, and listen to their viewpoints. Try to take a walk in other people's shoes. You might begin to appreciate the difficulty of their journey, which will help you better understand this Natural Force and its powerful influence on others.

Honesty Is the Best Policy

Equity will probably always be a source of conflict in organizations. Competitive market conditions for recruiting and retaining top talent, even during times of a weak economy, continue to widen the salary gap between an organization's upper-level employees and everyone else. Creating a more democratic organizational culture is not necessarily the most effective and successful business strategy. Organizations may be kidding themselves if they try to describe their operating philosophy as democratic when it simply may not be possible to conduct business in this way. Such claims may result in worsening the credibility gap. It is better to be honest with yourself and your employees and admit that things may not always be fair. This is not to say that organizations should stop working toward greater equity; they just need to be honest and realistic about these issues with all concerned.

Labor unions are quick to point out the often huge salary discrepancies between those at the tops of organizations and those at the lower levels. As it is unlikely that many CEOs would be willing to forgo their bonuses in the interests of appeasing their unionized workforces, this Natural Force is often best dealt with directly.

Take the example of one executive, who, when questioned about his high level of compensation at a meeting with hourly employees, simply stated, "I do make a lot of money. More than I ever thought I would. But I'll also say that my salary is commensurate with those of other executives at comparable companies. I work hard and achieve results that more than make up for my salary. If I weren't producing, I probably wouldn't have this job. I'm not ashamed of what I make, and I am proud of my accomplishments, which have put me in the position I hold today." No one in the room could find any fault with his statement. Because he acknowledged the existence of this perceived inequity and addressed it candidly, there were no further questions about his level of compensation.

In another example, a division of a large company was experiencing financial difficulties due to increased competition in the markets it served. At one time, this company had been the industry leader, enjoying unprecedented market share and profits. But as new competitors arrived on the scene and were able to produce the goods at significantly lower costs, particularly those for labor, the company saw its prices remain flat or even fall to levels that compromised its ability to operate profitably. The president of the division went to the factories where these products were made. He shared financial information with the workers, explaining the situation and the challenge the company was facing. He asked these workers to support the changes that were necessary to remain competitive and in business. He announced that there would be wage and benefits cuts for the next few years until the company's salaries were closer to those paid by the competition and the division could be profitable again. Although the workers didn't like the idea of having their wages and benefits cut, they understood the situation and accepted these actions. It seemed fair to them at the time. As a result of this and other changes, business improved and the division regained profitability.

Consequences of Underestimating the Equity Force

A problem occurred with the company mentioned above when it tried to keep wages frozen despite an improvement in business. Managers seriously miscalculated the Equity Natural Force. They thought that if they kept wages and benefits frozen for another year, the company could make up for lost profitability in the past. As mentioned previously, managers often underestimate their employees' ability to understand the business case. Employees know when business is good and when it is bad. They are the ones filling the orders, shipping the products, or providing the services. In this case, the workers knew the crisis was over. They became angry when they were told that their wages and benefits would remain frozen even though it was no longer a business necessity. They sought help from outside sources, calling in a labor union to organize their facilities. By miscalculating the power of the Equity Natural Force, the company had in effect handed its facilities over to the union.

Legislating Equity

When the Equity Natural Force fails, government intervention often follows. Inequity problems can result in potentially huge financial costs. In November 2000, Coca-Cola Co., the Atlanta-based soft drink giant, agreed to pay a record $192 million settlement in a racial discrimination suit involving pay, promotions, and performance appraisals.

A similar agreement was made by Texaco, Inc., in 1996, accompanied by what was at that time a landmark settlement of $176 million.

There are many laws and regulations designed to assure equity in organizations today. The Civil Rights Act of 1964 and later related legislation have enabled the government to become a watchdog over the Equity Natural Force in the workplace. The Americans with Disabilities Act of 1990 is designed to offer people with disabilities the same opportunity for gainful employment as those who are not disabled. The Family Medical Leave Act of 1993 allows employees with serious health conditions or who have family members with such conditions to take time off from work without being penalized. The Justice Department, which performs this watchdog function for the government, also monitors mergers, acquisitions, and other business dealings that could create an unfair advantage for a company. And all this is done in accord with the spirit of the Equity Natural Force.

Companies today struggle to comply with these laws while at the same time managing their businesses efficiently. These laws and regulations may sometimes seem overwhelming, making full compliance difficult, if not impossible. Many companies are struggling to cope not only with the spirit of the law but with the enormous administrative burden created by the regulations. Organizations must look at their promotion and compensation systems and make sure everyone is being given a fair and equal shot. These aims are highly desirable and go beyond basic legal or policy compliance. Without this discipline, this Natural Force can cause you to expend tremendous amounts of negative energy as equity tries to find some degree of equilibrium in your organization.

Creating Equity

The following guidelines can help you recognize the sources of real or perceived inequity in your organization and learn how to deal with them effectively.

Be Aware of the Gap Between Haves and Have-Nots

Managers in organizations must recognize this gap and remain constantly alert for those times when it begins to widen. Otherwise, it may grow to dangerous proportions.

Listen to What the Have-Nots Are Saying

There will always be people who feel they are getting a rotten deal and should have a bigger piece of the pie. Employees express their concerns about disparities, both perceived and real, in many different ways. Ignoring these messages can be a serious mistake. Every problem gives you advance warning; you just need to listen very carefully to hear what people are trying to say. If you do not, you may find yourself facing serious employee relations problems caused by the feelings of resentment your employees are harboring. The longer you wait to take action to correct a situation, the more you put your interests at risk.

Watch for Emerging Heroes

Occasionally a hero emerges to lead the struggle for the have-nots. Inequalities attract these kinds of champions, even if they are solely symbolic in nature. Symbolism often powers social-justice movements and causes. You need to be aware of such symbols in your organization. Do not try to change or even attack them as that will most likely serve to increase their appeal and influence. Rather, you must respect and understand these heroes. They are a powerful force in themselves.

Don't Be Fooled into Temporary Solutions

A problem may sometimes appear to be solved when it has only been interrupted or delayed for a time. It is similar to what happens when you paint over rust. The surface may look good for a while, but eventually the same problem begins to emerge. Don't be deceived into mistaking temporary fixes for permanent solutions just because people stop complaining about inequities. The inequities still exist; they just are not at center stage for the moment.

The following chart is a quick reference for the Equity Natural Force. It provides examples of ways in which to better manage or influence this force, specific actions or programs you might implement, and the impact these actions could have on employees.

Quick Reference for the Equity Natural Force

INFLUENCE ON NATURAL FORCE	MANAGEMENT ACTIONS	IMPACT ON EMPLOYEES
Policy announcements	Announce new policies and procedures.	Engenders fear of being adversely affected by new policies.
Appointments and promotions	Announce assignment of particular jobs and promotions.	Elicits positive or negative response according to their personal stake in the decision.
Business decisions	Announce future plans and company direction to the entire organization.	Stimulates thinking about whether this direction fits their long-term goals.
Reorganizations	Change the organization's structure and reporting relationships.	Creates a state of confusion and need to become focused on goals within the new structure.
Consolidations	Announce elimination of part(s) of the organization and combination of others.	Employees must find ways to do the same or even more work with fewer resources.
Salary administration	Distribute salaries in the way the organization believes will have the greatest impact on goals.	Makes salaries more of a disincentive than a motivator if a cause-and-effect relationship is not established between performance and rewards.
Demotions	Reduce employee responsibility and possibly salaries.	Creates fear of future negative consequences and fosters a protective mode rather than a productive one.
Benefits changes	Reduce benefits.	Creates a feeling that something of value has been taken away from them.
Budget cutbacks	Reduce resources, possibly saving money in the longer term.	May cause frustration because they have fewer resources with which to perform their jobs, making work more difficult.
Assignments	Assign responsibilities to high performers and certain others to lower performers.	Employees read a great deal into the type and nature of assignments they receive.

Performance

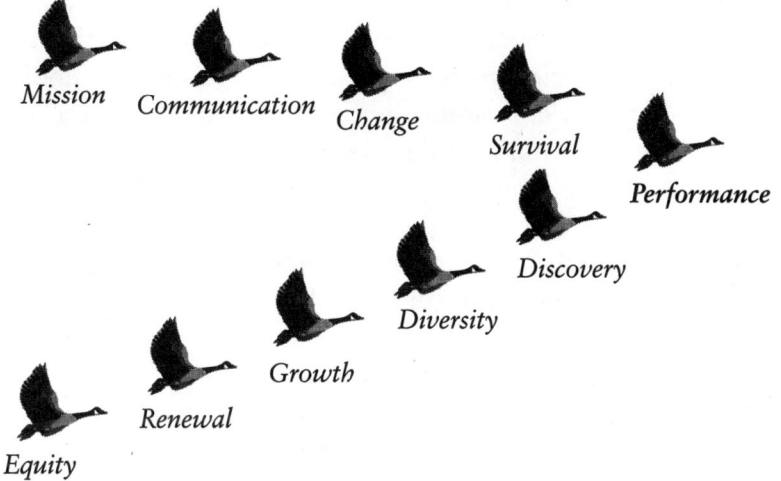

Mission *Communication* *Change* *Survival* *Performance* *Discovery* *Diversity* *Growth* *Renewal* *Equity*

LAWS OF THE PERFORMANCE NATURAL FORCE

- The predicted winner doesn't always prevail.

- Competitors help you perform at higher levels.

- It's important to know who your real competitors are.

- Performance is often a matter of systems design.

- Your method of measuring performance is critical to your results.

People are always striving to improve their lives, and they measure the factors that contribute to bettering their situations even if these factors are not within their control. If channeled correctly, this Natural Force can help everyone in the organization reach greater levels of performance. It is the Natural Force of Performance that sets the standards.

The Predicted Winner Doesn't Always Prevail

As in the biblical story of David and Goliath, the projected winner doesn't always defeat his or her rival. Everyone loves to see the underdog rise up from the bottom of the heap to stand on the victory platform. The 1968 World Series champions, the New York Mets, were considered a modern-day miracle when they won the pennant after enduring years of endless jokes about their poor performance on the field. Investors love to find underperforming stocks that most people haven't yet discovered, those with big potential to be successful in the future.

Competitors Help You Perform at Higher Levels

Capitalism is based on competition and has created the most prosperous society the world has ever seen. Natural competition allows the system to work more efficiently and reach greater levels of performance. We don't usually think of our rivals as allies, but in actuality they are often responsible for our greatest accomplishments. Their very existence motivates us to perform feats that we may never have thought possible. You probably won't be sending your competitors a thank-you note for their help in motivating your organization, yet they do force you to accomplish more.

Competition becomes a call to action that can't be ignored. If you don't answer this call, you will go out of business. It seizes everyone's attention at all levels of the organization. Competition can become a unifying force in the organization, just as a nation comes together to concentrate on winning a war against an enemy who threatens its existence. This Natural Force drove the United States and its allies to greater performance levels during World War II in their efforts to defeat Japan and Germany. In the early 1980s, Lee Iacocca effectively utilized the Performance Natural Force as

Chrysler's commander in chief, leading the battle against his company's enemy, the foreign import car. Just think about how many improvements in your organization's products or services were a result of efforts to keep up with or stay ahead of the competition. We don't always realize that we need our competitors to help keep us moving in the right direction.

It's Important to Know Who Your Real Competitors Are

When infighting begins in an organization, the only true winner is the *real* competition—those other companies that are trying to take away your customers. Employees need to know that the real competition is not some other department with which they have to share limited resources or the peers they are constantly battling with over petty issues. You are all on the same side, even though it is easy to lose sight of that fact. This Natural Force has a tendency to make every challenging situation into a competition.

Performance Is Often a Matter of Systems Design

Many managers become frustrated when they see constant infighting among their employees. They often give speech after speech on the need for teamwork and cooperation in the workplace in an attempt to change their employees' behavior. But they may be blaming the wrong people. The managers themselves are more likely causing the problem, because employees' behaviors are usually a result of their work environment. The system itself may be responsible for their competitive tendencies. Perhaps internal competition is unintentionally built into the system.

For example, say you have established systems designed to recognize the outstanding performance of a single individual, department, or even division of the organization. Sounds like a good idea, right? Well, maybe not. What really happens when a winner begins to emerge under these circumstances? If Crew 1 is far ahead of the other crews for a production contest in which the winner receives a reward that's perceived as valuable, what happens to the motivation, not to mention the morale, of the other crews? Obviously, they will not be very motivated or productive if they see inevitable defeat ahead. They may even become counterproductive. With nothing to lose, they may let output fall off its normal level. Nobody wants to work for a lost cause. Systems set up as "winner takes all" motivate only the winners, but there are many others in the organization who must remain motivated and productive. The solution is to set up incentive systems in which everyone can win. Rather than establishing "winner takes all" performance goals, set one that gives all workers the chance to reach desired performance levels of their own. That way, they won't be dragged down by someone else's performance. Under the new system, everyone can be a winner.

Your Method of Measuring Performance Is Critical to Your Results

Your performance measures can also be a factor in how well the system motivates employees to achieve certain goals. In many ways, you get what you measure. Strangely, numbers often tell you exactly what you want to hear—regardless of performance.

Too much emphasis on certain numbers may cause other areas to suffer. For example, in a warehouse operation in the Southeast, a large wholesale fruit distributor measured the output of each of the three shifts that worked during harvest season. The warehouse manager created what he thought was an incentive program by offering a financial bonus to the shift that loaded the most fruit per week. Output was measured by the weight of the trucks carrying the fruit at the end of each shift. In response to this program, employees began putting partially filled containers of fruit on the trucks near the end of their shifts, receiving credit for the pounds they'd loaded and preventing the next shift from claiming credit for the work they'd done. This created a nightmare, not only for warehouses that received the shipments and had to repack the partial crates to make full ones, but also for Accounting, which had to figure out how to credit the partially filled containers. All of these problems resulted from the company's incentive system, which was supposed to improve performance.

Instead, the distributor should have set up a performance measurement system based on 24 hours, not on shift-by-shift increments. This kind of system would be much more conducive to cooperation and collaboration among the shifts. Crews would be measured collectively rather than individually, giving them a reason to try to help one another. Leaving partially filled containers for the oncoming shift would no longer be considered counterproductive or self-defeating, and crews would be more likely to find ways of working efficiently and effectively together. One crew might do certain things to give the next crew a quicker start and thus increase its production. This simple change in the method of measuring performance would make teamwork and cooperation much more likely among the crews and throughout the organization. It would also reduce quality and accounting problems.

Managing Performance

Performance management involves controlling factors in the workplace that maximize employee performance. You might think that performance management focuses directly on the performance of employees; if someone doesn't perform up to standards, something should be done, such as disciplining or even discharging the employee. But think about how well that approach would have worked in our example of the fruit distributor's operation.

What if the warehouse manager had retained the original measurement and incentive system but began enforcing disciplinary action every time he found out an employee had loaded a partial container of fruit for shipment? Employees would still have been motivated to load as many pounds as possible during their shifts, but they probably would have applied their ingenuity to finding other ways of maximizing their shift's output at the expense of the other crews. Would this really have been the best use of the employees' creativity and energy? Until the warehouse corrected the problem in its reinforcement measurement system, the company had nothing to gain from punishing employees for trying to maximize their rewards by working within this system. More often than not, performance problems are a failure of the system, not of the employee, as when leadership unwittingly sets up performance systems that have failure built in.

Reinforce Behavior That Supports Organizational Goals

Performance systems are too often based on disincentives rather than on rewards. Employees often receive this message: "If you don't hear anything, you're doing just fine, but if you screw up, we'll let you know—big time!" Effective performance management systems are usually based on positive reinforcement, through feedback and incentives, of desired behaviors—those that support the organization's goals. Managers must be careful not to reinforce behaviors that do not support these goals. In the case of the fruit distribution center, management should cease rewarding the wrong behaviors (shipping partial containers) and reinforce the desired ones (working together across shifts). Ultimately, you will find that you get exactly what you reinforce, whether you are doing it intentionally or not.

We sometimes mix up rewards and punishments. Take, for example, a company that deals with an employee who is often absent from work by issuing warnings, which escalate to more serious action when ignored. This action often comes in the form of suspension from work, which is probably more reinforcement than punishment. The employee already has a propensity to take time off, and the company has just given him or her more time off. If managers really want to punish this employee, they should add hours to the work schedule instead! The point is that you need to think about the real impact of your decisions and actions on your employees. Are you setting up systems that will achieve what you hope to achieve, or are you creating incentives for counterproductive behaviors? You can manage performance much better if you stop rewarding the wrong behaviors and start setting up reinforcements for desired behaviors in the workplace.

Maintain Consistent Performance Standards

Too often, organizations set up systems to tap into this Natural Force in response to circumstances or situations. For example, maybe the marketing department wants to meet sales quotas before the end of the month or quarter, so management sets up temporary programs designed to spike performance for a certain time period. But reaching this performance level could be counterproductive, particularly if the department is borrowing from tomorrow's sales by enticing customers to make purchases earlier in the cycle. It is like eating tomorrow's lunch. This doesn't really improve performance in the long run; it only provides short-term comfort and a sense of false security. This is the inherent problem with the quarter-to-quarter performance-based systems most companies use today. Long-term goals are constantly taking a backseat to quarterly profit reports in an attempt to persuade financial analysts to look favorably on the company for their next buy or sell recommendation.

Achieving performance consistency is ultimately more productive than sporadic success, which, due to its inconsistent nature, may cause many anxious moments for those who are accountable for the organization's performance. It can be more important to keep performance levels consistent in the long run than to achieve temporary success, no matter how significant. Stock prices that soar to unbelievable heights can fall with the same abruptness.

Set Conditions for Higher Levels of Performance

The world of sports provides us with excellent examples of channeling the Performance Natural Force into record-breaking achievements. In this arena, the right conditions must exist before these higher levels of performance can be reached. Elements such as proper training, nutrition, instruction, conditioning, and equipment help optimize performance to progressively higher levels. The difference between one team and another may boil down to the coach's approach to resource management and the timing of decisions. It may also be a function of performance standards. Legendary coaches like Vince Lombardi are famous for the work ethic they instilled in their players and their desire to be winners. If you set your goals low, you can never expect to be a champion. As Lombardi said, "Winning isn't everything; it's the only thing." Coach Lombardi not only believed this; he also inspired his players to believe they could be winners.

Narrow the Performance Gaps

A *performance gap* is the distance between performance and potential. If there is a performance gap within an organization, it means that a resource is not being fully utilized. This resource could include people, equipment, processes, intellectual property, and markets. Whatever it is, if it is not being used, it is being wasted. The best-managed organizations are those that narrow this gap as much as possible. Just how narrow could be as much a function of your performance standard as of any other factor. What level of performance do you expect and think possible either from your organization or in those areas for which you are responsible? In many ways, you determine this gap.

Think about the extraordinarily talented golfer Tiger Woods. He won his first major championship by completely dominating the 1997 Masters Tournament. The entire world was in awe of this young man's incredible accomplishments and ability. Everyone, that is, except Woods himself. He studied his swing on videotape and wasn't satisfied. He saw a performance gap between his actual and his potential swing. Although everyone else thought he was at the top of his game, he knew he could do better. He sought to close the performance gap and worked on his swing until he felt it was as close to perfection as possible, at least for the time being. When he resurfaced on the leader boards of major golf tournaments after retooling his swing, everyone began to realize his true potential. Only time will tell what his ultimate golfing performance level will be. One thing we do know: his performance gap will be as narrow as is humanly possible.

What is the performance gap in your organization? Are you satisfied with this gap as it exists today, or could it be smaller? How many resources are not being utilized to their highest potential? The difference between top performers and the rest of the pack may be a matter not of resource availability or allocation but rather of how effectively these resources are managed.

The Performance Natural Force is most powerful when it is challenged. If you don't challenge all members of the organization to reach their performance potential, they will find ways to express these energies by different means. They may develop counterproductive behaviors that are somehow sustained or reinforced by the system itself. People want an opportunity to perform well and gain recognition for their accomplishments. They enjoy being part of an excellent operation and want to contribute to its success. Understanding this Natural Force will increase your ability to provide a work environment that enables everyone to meet his or her performance goals in the future. By doing this, you will make the gap between potential and performance as narrow as possible.

Understand the Difference Between Competition and Collaboration

The challenge in organizations is to channel natural competitive feelings into energy that raises the performance bar without becoming self-destructive. For example, if different divisions or departments of an organization compete against one another to the point that collaboration no longer exists, the company is fighting itself, and the actual winner is the real competition—those other companies that are trying to take away customers. If, however, the Performance Natural Force is properly harnessed and applied to the right objectives, it can move the organization toward greater accomplishments.

Organizations need to develop the communication and educational processes that keep employees at every level focused on the real competition and intent on maximizing this Natural Force. All members of the organization must be able to recognize those situations in which either challenge or collaboration is appropriate and necessary between departments; they must also understand that infighting weakens their own organization to the point that it is no longer competitive with outside groups. When you try to win too much and too often, you may find that you have actually lost in the end. This Natural Force will make you less competitive if your efforts are targeting the wrong things.

Characteristics of Top-Performing Organizations

Your organization's overall performance should be important to all your employees as well as to your stockholders and other sponsors. However, performance doesn't always meet expectations, and this can lead to serious consequences, such as demotivation and counterproductive behaviors.

Managers should look not only at bottom-line results but at factors that contribute to high performance levels for their organizations. The following twelve characteristics have been identified as contributing to the success of top-performing organizations. Fostering these characteristics in your organization will help you begin to understand what you need to do to increase performance.

Innovation

Top performers typically are innovators. They are constantly finding new and innovative ways not only to produce or deliver familiar products but to serve their customers. Many companies claim to be innovators, but there are generally very few truly innovative ideas that aren't copies of something that already exists. To innovate is to be a leader. Innovation gives a company a head start. It usually takes some amount of time before competitors catch up to the innovator, and by the time they do, the innovator is on to something new and different. Innovators create the future; followers spend all their time trying to catch up or keep up with the pace set by the innovators.

Confidence

No one is guaranteed success, particularly in light of today's economy. Top performers have confidence in themselves but never take success for granted. They realize that confidence is something you have to earn every day in business. Your customers, employees, suppliers, and stockholders must have confidence in your ability to do everything you can do to remain successful, regardless of the situation.

Resilience

The fall of the dot-com industry didn't cause every high-tech company to fail. Many even found ways to thrive despite the many obstacles to continued success they encountered in the wake of the declines all around them. These are the true high performers in their industry. Success was widespread when the dot-com industry was on the rise, but only a few organizations sustained that level of performance during the decline. Part of being resilient is being ready for the unpredictable. You need to plan ahead for success as well as for slumps in the economy and business cycle.

Consistency

Resilience leads to consistency. Most dot-com companies lacked any consistent pattern of success in their performance, which was sporadic at best. They did well only under the optimum conditions for their business. In comparison, many of the old-economy industries had long histories, some even going back a century or more, of steady good performance. Consistent good performance ultimately trumps temporary high performance. It may not sound as sexy as being an overnight business wonder, but it will keep on paying the bills into the future.

Controlled Aggressiveness

Aggressiveness can be both a strength and a liability to an organization. Many promising companies end up bankrupt because they were too aggressive in their investment and acquisition strategies. Aggressiveness serves best when it is controlled and well applied; being reckless when it comes to committing the organization's assets will almost certainly lead to disaster. Everyone has a story about a missed opportunity, and there may truly be no way to avoid this experience, but investing in every opportunity just because it might someday be the one that got away is not the answer.

Self-Knowledge

It is important to know your areas of strength and weakness. Don't try to be something you are not. Many companies seeking to diversify their portfolios venture into businesses about which they know nothing and in which they have little or no expertise. Although this may be a successful strategy under some circumstances, there are many potential land mines along the way. You are more likely to be successful when you are doing what you do best. A successful company builds on its core business, growing in areas related to its field of knowledge and expertise. If you want to introduce something new, then proceed in phases. It's a competitive world out there, and even those who are very good at certain things will fail. Building on what you already know how to do will put you out in front of the competition.

Economic Balance

This is what might be called the best of both worlds. The new economy is represented by high-technology businesses such as those found on the NASDAQ, while the old economy is represented by more traditional industries, like the ones listed in the Dow Jones Industrial average. A company can achieve balance by being involved in both economies. This will strengthen the organization's ability to weather the economic storms that tend to blow in on a regular basis.

In addition, both types of economies bring desirable elements into the organization. Technology can help prepare you to meet the increasing demands of the marketplace; traditional businesses may keep you grounded in your fundamental business approach. The sides nicely balance each other, complementing their separate strengths and compensating for their weaknesses. The merger of AOL and Time Warner in early 2001 is an excellent example of the marriage of the two economies. Consumers will benefit from Time Warner's large array of online media properties, while AOL's sites will have access to innumerable resources, with sports sites drawing on articles and pictures from *Sports Illustrated,* music sites tapping into the Warner Bros. music library, and news sites connecting to stories from *Time* magazine and CNN.

Good Timing

It seems that timing is everything. Poor timing can be one of the most disastrous circumstances for a new endeavor, but sometimes it just can't be helped. You have no way of knowing what other events or circumstances are going to occur that might put your plans in jeopardy or lead to certain failure. However, this fatalistic approach may not always be justified. You may occasionally be able to discern probabilities using a little intuition and investigation. Research can tell you a great deal or at least tip you off that the timing of your plans may not be right. Good timing doesn't always happen strictly by chance. It usually isn't an accident when someone is in the right place at the right time.

Focused Strategy

A focused strategy that is available to everyone in the organization is a vital part of achieving your desired performance levels. The most successful companies are frequently those with the clearest vision of how they are going to reach their goals. Everyone needs to stay focused on the organization's direction and should understand his or her role in the overall strategy. Another important skill is the ability to anticipate market changes; top-performing companies are usually willing to modify their strategies as necessary to adjust to changes in the marketplace.

Customer Focus

It is easy to get so caught up in the everyday struggle to manage a business that you forget what it is really all about. It's the customer, dummy! If your organization is concentrating on anything other than the customer, you are expending energy in the wrong place. The customer is the reason you are in business. Without the customer, you go out of business. Every system, job, procedure, process, and policy must consider the customer to some degree in its design. Knowledge about the customer should run throughout the entire organization and not be restricted to the sales and marketing departments.

Ability to Learn from Failure

Failure is sometimes the best thing that can happen. It can lead you to great opportunities and may serve as a wake-up call to the organization or to certain individuals that something needs to be done. Without this call, the same conditions that create problems will continue to adversely affect the organization. You need to look at the reasons behind failure and begin the process of making changes so that you can prevent it from happening again. If you don't, all the upset and hassle that come with failure will truly be for nothing. Failure can be an excellent teacher, but you have to pay attention to its lessons.

Luck

There is an old saying, "It is better to be lucky than good." Although this may be true, you can't always count on luck. On the other hand, luck can't be completely ignored either. It occasionally does play a part. You can do everything right and deserve to be successful but still fail due to some factor beyond your control. You may see others succeed because of nothing they did or get breaks they didn't really deserve. Luck can be very unpredictable—it comes and goes as it pleases. All you can do is hope for the best in terms of luck and do everything you can to control those factors that are within your grasp.

But did you ever wonder why some people seem to have all the luck? Perhaps they were born under the right star, or maybe they are doing something that puts them in the best position to benefit from luck if it favors them. In many ways, you make your own luck. Be sure you are in the best position to take advantage of a lucky break if it should come your way.

The following chart is a quick reference for the Performance Natural Force. It provides examples of ways in which to better manage or influence this force, specific actions or programs you might implement, and the impact these actions could have on employees.

Quick Reference for the Performance Natural Force		
INFLUENCE ON NATURAL FORCE	MANAGEMENT ACTIONS	IMPACT ON EMPLOYEES
Incentives and awards	Offer incentives to encourage employees to perform at higher levels.	Motivates if people feel the goals are reasonable; otherwise, programs have little impact.
Performance feedback	Give performance feedback as a way of helping employees grow and develop in their careers.	Can be helpful if provided consistently and in a timely manner. If not, employees won't get the connection.
Motivational programs	Design programs to inspire employees to work harder.	Motivates if honest and up front about the intended outcome.
New equipment	Invest in equipment designed to produce greater levels of work.	Improves performance without creating many other employee issues.
Process improvement	Study and modify processes in order to produce highest-level performance possible.	Works best with input from those closest to the process.
Competitive analysis	Compare organization with outside competitors.	Increases understanding of who the competition is and how to remain competitive.
Cost cutting	Cut costs wherever possible so as to produce greater profit returns on sales dollars.	Causes frustration when expenditures that make their jobs easier are eliminated.
Performance goals	Establish desired performance goals and monitor progress.	Helps them feel connected to these goals through accountabilities or rewards, or preferably both.

Discovery

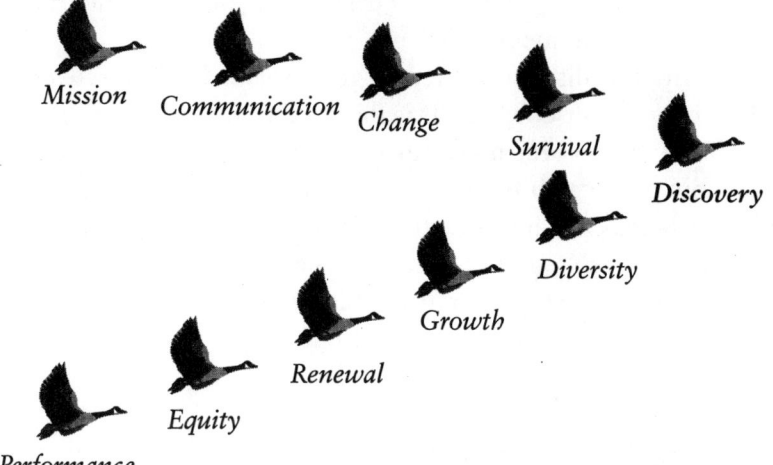

Mission Communication Change

Survival

Discovery

Diversity

Growth

Renewal

Equity

Performance

LAWS OF THE DISCOVERY
NATURAL FORCE

- The need for discovery will always exist.

- Discovery leads to obsolescence.

- Discovery needs to be nurtured.

- Crisis drives discovery.

- Discovery has its downside.

This Natural Force is the one that leads to inventing a better mousetrap. No matter how good the current technology for catching mice may be, someone is always looking for a better method. However, there are significant challenges that can interfere with the natural progression of the process. The most effective managers find ways to remove these barriers to discovery.

The Need for Discovery Will Always Exist

Progress doesn't stop, even if everyone is perfectly satisfied with the current state of affairs. Discovery creates needs. Before the Internet and e-mail were introduced, consumers didn't realize they couldn't function without being able to send messages or electronic files to someone else instantaneously.

Furthermore, discovery creates discovery. Every discovery is based on previous discoveries. It is the combining of discoveries that makes this Natural Force most powerful. We sometimes have to wait for technology to catch up with an idea that's ahead of its time, but in other instances it is just a matter of putting the right combination of ideas or concepts together, which is what happened with the Palm Pilot and the Internet. Either way, this synergistic approach is the key to discovering the mysteries and challenges that lie ahead for mankind.

Discovery Leads to Obsolescence

As is true of many other organizational forces, discovery can become a political process in the sense that discovery leads to obsolescence. Obsolescence is a problem to people who have invested their careers or perhaps their fortunes in something and don't want to see it disappear. Examples abound, such as the automobile replacing the horse and buggy, television replacing radio as the primary form of home entertainment, the personal computer replacing the electric typewriter, and e-mail replacing many forms of paper documents. Each of these discoveries met with some level of resistance because customs, old processes, and familiar lifestyles had to be pushed aside for the innovation. This reaction is natural and to be expected.

Likewise, you can find outdated manufacturing processes, antiquated procedures, or obsolete products lingering on far beyond their useful life span in any organization. This often has to do with what are referred to as *sunk costs*. Sunk costs are previously invested money that someone doesn't want to see go to waste. It is the organizational equivalent of "throwing good money after bad." Progress often gets bogged down at this point in the discovery process.

Resistance to discovery is surmountable, even if it may not seem possible at first. Discovery is a powerful force once it is unleashed. People will accept something new, but that may not happen until they're ready or circumstances dictate their acceptance. For example, car buyers weren't particularly interested in fuel-efficient technology for automobiles until the cost of gasoline began to rise in the 1970s. An idea may be ahead of its time and requires the right conditions before it is accepted.

Discovery Needs to Be Nurtured

This Natural Force must be nurtured so that it can propel the organization toward tomorrow's revelations—usually much easier said than done. All organizations contain a certain amount of inertia, which resists the introduction of anything new. People might come up with countless reasons why the new discovery will cause far too much turmoil or cost too much to introduce. The best thing to do, some will argue, is to stick with the status quo instead of trying a newfangled procedure or product that is probably doomed to failure.

Advocating change through discovery may make you feel like a political dissident or an anarchist within the organization. It takes a great deal of courage to promote the Discovery Natural Force against the opposition of powerful people in the organization. But this is a force that can't be stopped, and it will eventually break through every barrier in its way. Interestingly enough, those who resisted the discovery most strenuously may one day embrace its inevitable arrival as if they had supported and believed in it all along. They are probably heeding the advice of the old saying "If you can't beat 'em, join 'em." All you can or should do at that point is smile to yourself and remember that this Natural Force is much more powerful than anyone's ability to stop it. If something needs to be discovered, it will be found by someone, someday. No force on earth can stop that from happening.

Crisis Drives Discovery

Many of the most important discoveries of our time have occurred as solutions to crises. For example, the polio vaccine was developed in the 1950s to meet an urgent public-health need. External threats or challenges may also spur discovery. The development of the atomic bomb near the end of World War II and our nation's determination beginning in the 1960s to become the leader in the space race are examples of an entire country responding to this Natural Force.

Discovery is most important when it is needed most urgently. Organizations facing crises are more receptive to discovery than they are under normal conditions. Everyone begins saying things like "Something's got to change around here." Unfortunately, this receptivity usually comes only after it has become painfully obvious that something new is required to deal with the situation. Recent problems can make an organization more cautious and conservative in its willingness to accept risk.

Discovery Has Its Downside

Believe it or not, there is an argument against discovery. Mistakes can be made, and discoveries may not turn out as expected; trying to achieve competitive advantage has caused company after company to pour millions, sometimes even billions, of dollars into the proverbial black hole, only to see little or no return on their investment. These unfortunate possibilities are at least partially responsible for most bad investment decisions, process changes that ultimately fail, and needless business collapses. Yet, the potential downside does not take away from the strength of this Natural Force; on the contrary, it emphasizes the force's power. It is the misdirected Natural Force of Discovery that is responsible for these mistakes.

Recognizing Signs of Resistance to Discovery

You may find it necessary to become the discovery's strongest advocate and sponsor. If you don't, quite possibly no one else will. If you truly believe in the discovery, don't stop trying to get it implemented. Resistance is sometimes disguised as a rationale for rejecting the introduction of something new. You need to be able to separate the reasons that are legitimate from those that are not. The following are a few telltale signs that resistance to discovery may be occurring in your organization.

Fear

Let's face it—discovery changes things, and people who fear changes have tried to stop discoveries since the beginning of time. The introduction of something new will upset the status quo or some balance of power that they currently enjoy and that they feel is being threatened. You can easily be seduced by pleas to leave things alone. "Don't rock the boat or you might send someone or something of importance down with the ship" becomes the theme of the day. Fear may score a more direct hit on discovery, as when funding or budgets suddenly dry up just as a new discovery appears to be gaining some momentum and acceptance.

Disinterest

A key supporter may suddenly lose interest in or oppose the discovery. Perhaps you just need to wait for the discovery's moment to arrive. This may not be the right time and place for it.

Negative Atmosphere

When something associated with but not directly related to the discovery fails, it may create doubts about the validity of the discovery itself. Suddenly, everyone is wondering what else might go wrong. If this is the situation, you need to make sure that you understand the difference between what just happened and the chances that this failure will be repeated with the discovery. If there is no correlation, you must communicate this fact to the key decision makers.

Lack of Attention

As a collective entity, an organization must concentrate on many new things, and it is important to understand that a particular discovery isn't the only item competing for everyone's attention. At the same time, you don't want an important discovery to be swept away by the tide of new ideas swarming into the organization, particularly if the discovery is of significance.

Discovery Lessons Learned from the Dot-Com Industry

A postmortem look at the dot-com industry of the early 2000s reveals a number of lessons about the Discovery Natural Force. The first and foremost has to do with the speed at which discovery is introduced. History often proves that the faster a discovery emerges, the swifter its departure will be. There may indeed be no such thing as overnight success—at least not one that sustains itself beyond the short term.

If something is easily imitated, there is no competitive advantage. It became far too easy for anyone who could raise enough capital to start his or her own dot-com venture and participate in the latest business fad promising instant success and wealth. Unfortunately, so many would-be entrepreneurs jumped on the dot-com bandwagon that it collapsed under its own weight.

Ultimately, people will always have to consider basic principles and follow certain rules in order to achieve success. If you believe success can be gained in any other way, you will be disappointed unless you consistently have the insight and vision to liquidate your investments at the peak of their profitability.

Basic Business Models Are Still Valid

There must be a correlation between spending and return on spending, even when it comes to a new discovery. You can't make discoveries without some investment—after all, they do cost money—but you can't pour money down a sinkhole and expect to continue attracting investors, much less survive for very long. Discovery alone can't keep a failing enterprise afloat; bottom-line results are still important. Every business or organization must justify its existence.

A discovery must eventually pay off on the investments made to maintain its existence. Seen in terms of a business model, the projected return on investment has to fulfill the organization's spending justifications. Otherwise, no matter how significant the discovery, if it doesn't eventually support the bottom line, it won't survive in most business situations. Before pursuing any discovery, you should make an honest attempt to determine whether it will meet the justification criteria of your organization.

Choose Expensive Technologies Carefully

Choose expensive technologies as if your business depended on them—because it does. An unwise investment in expensive technology could virtually bankrupt your company if it doesn't work. Don't decide to "bet the farm" based on a hunch or untested speculation. Experiment, perform a pilot study, conduct research, and do whatever is necessary to justify a technology investment for the discovery. What if the technology costs more to implement than you are willing to spend? Do you still want to go forward with this discovery? You must be clear on the price you are willing to pay for bringing discoveries to fruition as well as the consequences of these costs. It's important to develop an exit strategy and identify the point in the overall project plan at which you should terminate development if certain benchmarks are not met.

Understand When Discovery Is Not Needed

Sometimes we keep looking for that better mousetrap even though the current technology is just fine. Going online with certain businesses just didn't make sense—maybe someday, but not today. There may be some factors that prevent the discovery from working effectively. These factors could have such a limiting effect that they eventually negate any gains created by the discovery. For example, many online retailers found that despite the efficiency of Internet buying, shipping to the customer was still a function of the traditional ground transportation services available in their local areas. Frustrated by delays, many retail customers found it was quicker to go to the nearest mall and purchase the item than to wait for it to be delivered by mail. All the benefits of technology are for naught if a bottleneck is still part of the system. An online retailer might ship a piece of clothing out the door in less than 24 hours, but if it gets stuck on the delivery truck for a week, the customer will be unhappy with the clothing distributor.

Discovery Alone Will Not Bring Success

Being first to market is a huge competitive advantage when something new is discovered. Great fortunes can be made during the time when a company is in possession of an exclusive discovery and the competition is still offering yesterday's technology to a market that is clamoring for the next big thing. However, organizations often confuse the concepts of "first to market" and "creating the latest discovery." It is a huge advantage to discover something before everyone else knows about it, but you must be able to succeed at selling it as well. Making the discovery doesn't mean that you will be able to bring it to market and reap its rewards. This involves an entirely different set of skills. You might be great at discovery but poor at marketing. Make sure you are involving the right people during the various stages of the overall process. Don't lose discovery's competitive edge through poor sales and marketing implementation.

Don't Rest on Your Laurels

You should also accept the fact that you might have just happened to make the right discovery at the right time and under the right circumstances. This doesn't necessarily mean that you are suddenly a business genius. Don't get too full of yourself and assume you can maintain your unique competitive advantage for an extended period of time. The party may not last forever. Reap the rewards while they last, but begin planning for reality to return to your bottom line sooner or later (probably sooner) by focusing on more realistic goals for the future. With realistic strategic planning, this success can lead to future successes. If only more dot-com overnight wonders had taken this advice, they might still be in business today.

Experience Still Counts

Most of all, you need to surround yourself with talented people who know how to turn discovery into profit. The return of traditional industries to the business forefront reaffirms the value of experience in the long run. Not having managers who would remind them of basic business principles such as the need for revenue to exceed costs was perhaps the biggest mistake made by many dot-com companies during their heyday. You can get by without making a profit for a while, but without income the company will soon fall apart like a house of cards. You can't cheat such a basic rule of business any more than you can hold off a Natural Force for very long. In the end, Natural Forces will prevail and put things in their rightful order.

Managing Discovery

Discovery can be a very fickle force. It is easily misjudged or mismanaged. It can thrust you ahead on the wave of the next big thing or leave you bankrupt because of a sudden and unpredictable change in direction. Management's goal should be to lead the organization to the position of greatest potential for discovery.

Sometimes that perfect opportunity comes your way, and other times you must find it yourself. Whatever the case, it will probably be up to you to make the most of it. In business, you are seldom presented with a perfect discovery scenario; there are always obstacles and problems to be overcome. Your job is to manage the discovery so that it will lead to success instead of being remembered as a promising but unfeasible idea.

Create an Atmosphere Conducive to Discovery

Organizations must be ready and willing to accept this Natural Force when it appears, for if they wait too long, they might miss the kinds of great opportunities that knock on a company's door but once. Study how your systems, practices, feedback, and so on deal with the Natural Force of Discovery. Do your organization's responses to new ideas kill them instantly, or do they encourage and reinforce discovery?

Many organizations sponsor incentive or suggestion programs designed to encourage employees to bring forward their ideas on workplace or business improvements. However, organizations often become frustrated with these programs, citing lack of value or return on the projects suggested by employees. For example, one project might involve moving something from point A to point B, and a later project will suggest that it be moved back. Obviously, these types of projects don't enhance discovery in the organization; they only tell everyone that the object really did belong at point A all along. This is also part of the discovery process. You must be willing to accept the good with the bad, the valuable with the useless. If you receive only one really significant suggestion through your program, it will all be worthwhile.

Every discovery doesn't have to be a grand-slam home run—even a base hit can lead to runs if you keep the momentum of discovery moving forward. Discovery is often more about finding new ways of doing old things than about coming up with an entirely new approach. It does not take a paradigm shift to make a discovery significant. Simply improving the lives of your customers in the smallest way can represent a significant discovery to them.

Don't forget that sometimes the unlikeliest of heroes can emerge to win the game. Don't stop giving people the chance to play in the discovery game. You just might find that diamond in the rough, which you had forgotten about or never given the chance to shine.

Be Willing to Make Tough Decisions

Leadership needs to make the tough decisions. Will you let a discovery go by and hope that it wasn't a missed opportunity? Or should you go ahead and try to capitalize on it? When you step up to the decision-making plate, you never really know if you are going to swing at the wrong pitch or let that home-run ball pass you by. All you can do is knock the dust off your cleats and take your best swing.

Discovery drives an organization to make decisions that may or may not be right. Everyone knows that you sometimes have to make risky decisions. This is just part of life, but you must be able to make good decisions. The ability to identify the best bet is critical to making the right decision. Although jumping in too quickly can be a problem if you are not ready for discovery, delaying decision making until you are certain that the risks are minimal can also lead to failure.

Learn from Your Mistakes

Many business failures are caused by the pursuit of some discovery that drives an otherwise successful enterprise into bankruptcy. Someone may have thought that this discovery was going to be the next big thing or would move the company in the direction required for future success. In hindsight, it is always easy to see that some decisions were wrong for any number of reasons. Perhaps the company's research was inadequate, inaccurate, or biased, or the decision to proceed was based on someone's gut feeling, without having been given the appropriate thought or analysis.

You must consider every step along the journey of discovery as part of the learning process. Learning what doesn't work can be as valuable as learning what does. The most important part of discovery is gaining from your experiences. Unfortunately, these lessons often aren't recognized or remembered for very long. Institutional memory can be very short. Decision makers leave, and those who replace them may repeat the mistakes of the past. Watch out for the flip side of this coin, however. Just because something didn't work in the past doesn't mean it would not be effective under other circumstances.

Position Your Organization at the Point of Greatest Potential

A photographer puts himself in a particular time and place so he can get the perfect award-winning shot for that magazine cover. The photographer *creates the opportunity* for that fantastic picture; he doesn't just wait for it to happen. *National Geographic* photographer Dewitt Jones talks about this in his beautifully produced video *Everyday Creativity*. He says you can either hope to stumble on that moment and trust you are prepared to capitalize on the opportunity when it presents itself or try to place yourself in the position of greatest potential, where you can capitalize on new discoveries. If you rush to get your camera when the light is just right, you will probably be too late. Moreover, many other photographers may be there, setting up their cameras as well. You will then have to fight for position, and your competitive edge will be gone.

So let's say you have your camera and equipment ready and are waiting at what Jones describes as the "point of greatest potential," but it is cloudy and overcast that morning. You will have to come back the next day, or you will never take the great picture that ends up on that magazine cover and makes all the effort and expense worthwhile. You have to keep trying as long as possible. Think of how many times Thomas Edison repeated his experiments before he achieved his success. He never gave up or allowed failure to stop the discovery process.

No matter how sophisticated communications and technology become, discovery will always be as much an art as a science. There are no exact formulas for successful discovery. One thing is certain: like the photographer, you must be in the right place at the right time, prepared to capitalize on circumstances and events. Discovery may be as much about luck as anything else. Sometimes, the best discoveries occur when you are not really trying to find anything. You have to be alert to discovery even when you're not in the market.

Find Ways to Help Others Buy Into the Discovery

People may not always greet discovery with open arms. Change can be a bitter pill to swallow. Be patient with others as you lead discovery in your organization. Discovery may indeed make their lives easier and better, but the process can be a difficult road to travel. Help those who have taken a definite stand against discovery to find a graceful way to accept change. Give them a little extra time to get used to new ways and ideas. You will find that the process goes much more smoothly if you do.

Making the Most of Discovery Opportunities

When discovery does come, you need to keep a few things in mind in order to capitalize on the natural momentum of this force. The following suggestions will help you make the most of your opportunities for discovery.

Do Your Homework

Above all, you must do whatever research is required to prepare for the new product, idea, or process. The last thing you want is to invest your organization's resources in an idea that was doomed from the start. Many disasters can be avoided by doing a little more research before moving ahead. There are almost always warning signs when the situation truly warrants caution. Remember, the *Titanic* received reports of icebergs in the area that April evening, but the captain chose to ignore the warnings.

Give It a Test Run

You should test and retest your new product, idea, or process before moving forward. Run trials, conduct simulations or pilot projects, solicit opinions, collect data, or do whatever you can to determine the viability of the project beforehand. Even if you decide not to proceed, you will have gained valuable information during this data-collection phase, which may be useful later as you continue.

This is the time to analyze the data carefully. Take a long, hard look at your research before you decide to move ahead. Most important, keep an open mind about the project's viability during this evaluative stage. Don't slant the data with your preconceived opinions and desire to see the project move forward. This is often the weakest part of the discovery process in organizations. The data may clearly show that there are many inherent risks to a project, but nobody wants to hear this news. The facts are ignored or dismissed as irrelevant when they should be seriously considered. Once again, everyone seems to start playing "emperor's new clothes," afraid to speak the truth even when it is right in front of them.

Get Good Advice

There is a great deal of good advice available on almost any subject, and it can come from many different people and places. Sometimes, it is best to get advice from unconventional sources. For instance, instead of hiring a consultant, you might ask your customers for their thoughts on the project. They would certainly be a valuable resource for advice, as would your suppliers, employees, and stockholders. You can also get advice by accessing information that is readily available to you. For instance, think of ways in which you could use the Internet to acquire advice indirectly from sources such as your competitors, with whom you might not wish to share your plans. Perhaps they already have some experience with trying to do what you are considering, and you could benefit by not making their mistakes.

Support Development

You don't want to have a viable idea that becomes a poorly executed project. Make sure that the people you put in charge have the resources and support they need for successful implementation. Project sponsors need to stay in touch with the development team in order to provide emotional support and understand what is needed to keep moving ahead. Their involvement can be critical to the project's success.

Plan for Things to Go Wrong

Let's face it, you are going to have setbacks along the way to discovery. You need to build some contingencies into your project plan. It is probably a sure bet that you will need more time, money, or other resources than you originally estimated. It will be much easier to access these additional resources if they were built into the plan; surprising the project sponsors with requests for more funding or time is usually not an effective tactic.

Don't Abandon a Viable Project

Remember, anything can look like a failure when you're in the middle of it. It is easy to begin doubting the validity of a project when the inevitable problems begin to arise. But if you have done your homework, planned for a few bumps in the road, secured the needed support, and decided that you have a truly viable project, then you need to persevere. Many projects are abandoned before they have been given a fair chance to succeed, only to be picked up again at a later date and taken to completion. Before scrubbing a project and losing everything that has been put into it, make sure it deserves to be abandoned. If it does, then so be it. Every organization has its share of failures. Cut your losses and move on. Learn what you can from the experience so that it won't happen again in the future. On the other hand, if the project is worthwhile, take a step back and determine what needs to be done to get it headed in the right direction, and then act on what you have learned.

The following chart is a quick reference for the Discovery Natural Force. It provides examples of ways to better manage or influence this force, specific actions or programs you might implement, and the impact these actions could have on employees.

Quick Reference for the Discovery Natural Force		
INFLUENCE ON NATURAL FORCE	MANAGEMENT ACTIONS	IMPACT ON EMPLOYEES
Research and development	Invest capital resources in the discovery.	Shows that the organization is serious about discovery. Money often speaks louder than words.
Suggestion programs	Offer employees a way to share their discovery ideas.	Provides an outlet for employees' ideas. The program will be used to the extent that management reinforces their ideas.
Employee involvement	Sponsor programs that encourage employees to become more involved in decisions.	Fosters a sense of membership in decision-making and problem-solving processes.
Customer feedback	Establish tools for eliciting customer opinions on products and services.	Data from customer feedback enables employees to make appropriate adjustments.
Employee surveys	Establish tools for eliciting employee opinions about working for the organization.	Encourages a sense of contributing to management discovery process by sharing how they feel about working for the organization.
Consumer buying trends	Conduct studies to learn if customers are buying the latest discoveries.	May dictate job security and career growth for employees.
Costs	Institute measures designed to track the costs of discovery.	Employees are often the first to realize that a discovery is not justifying its existence. Managers should listen.
Organizational design	Review organizational structures in terms of their influence on the discovery process, which may lead to workplace redesign and relocations.	Serious frustration may result from an organizational design that is not conducive to discovery; employees feel that they are fighting a losing battle to be innovative.

Diversity

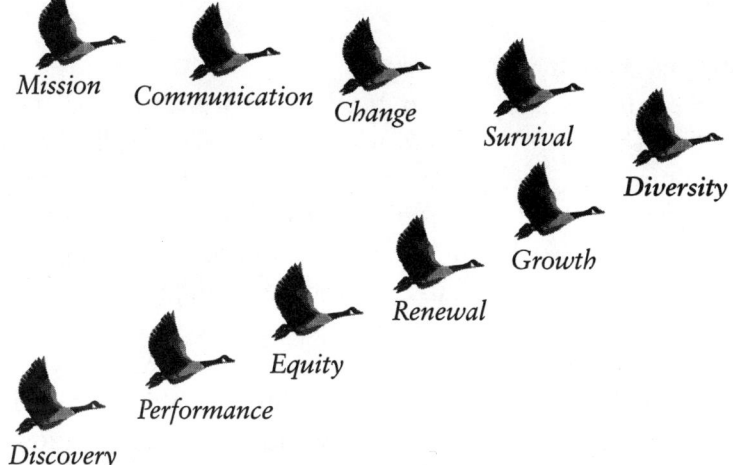

Mission Communication Change Survival Diversity Growth Renewal Equity Performance Discovery

LAWS OF THE DIVERSITY NATURAL FORCE

- Diversity can be a matter of survival.

- Actions speak louder than words.

- Diversity must be institutionalized.

Diversity makes people and their ideas unique. The world is becoming more and more diverse every day, and this Natural Force is rapidly carrying over into our organizations. Electronic communications and technology are giving us much greater access to one another, thus enabling us to better understand and accept our differences. Uniformity, conformity, and prejudicial thinking greatly hinder organization development and can be directly opposed to the Natural Force of Diversity. Diversity needs to be channeled so that it encourages, even celebrates, a broader spectrum of viewpoints. When this happens, you will be able to make better decisions that reflect input from a wider variety of people in your organization.

Diversity Can Be a Matter of Survival

Joel Barker, in his 2001 video *Wealth, Innovation, & Diversity: Putting Our Differences to Work in the 21st Century,* tells the story of two cultures that based their diets on the potato.

The first is Ireland in the mid-1800s. Over the preceding two centuries, the Irish bred all differences out of potatoes until they had the one "perfect" variety that appeared best suited to their needs. History testifies to the disastrous results of this decision. Because the Irish depended on only one strain of potato, they were vulnerable to a disease that affected this particular type, and when the blight wiped out the entire crop, they suffered famine and massive starvation.

In contrast, Barker tells of another culture that actually prospered from its potato diet several centuries earlier. The Incas, living in the Andes mountains between the 12th and 16th centuries in what is now Peru, sought to develop as many varieties of potato as they possibly could. They believed that growing many types of potato increased their chances of always having this important food source available, so they developed varieties of potatoes that thrived under all kinds of conditions—wet weather or dry, warm temperatures or cool. And if a disease or an insect destroyed one strain, chances were that the others, or at least some of them, would survive. By creating this diversity in their food supply, the Incas were less vulnerable to a single cause or event destroying their life-sustaining source of nourishment.

As illustrated by the potato stories, diversity is often a matter of survival. It is a necessary force that creates a variety of viewpoints, perspectives, and objectives in an organization. Tremendous value can be realized through practicing inclusion, as opposed to exclusion, of nontraditional backgrounds in organizational decision-making processes. Like-thinking can be one of the most dangerous ailments for an organization. Diversity of backgrounds, viewpoints, values, and interests, among many other areas, is needed instead. It is not a good thing when everyone gives the same answer, despite the organizational pressures favoring conformity.

Actions Speak Louder Than Words

"Walking the talk" is the real challenge for organizations, even those that have diversity programs. Diversity must be more than a public or employee relations tool. It should be more than just another buzz-word or a policy statement displayed on the wall. It has to have real meaning to the organization. Actions do speak louder than words. All the efforts to educate and promote these concepts in the organization can be negated by a single contradictory action or a pronouncement from management that appears inconsistent with the official diversity policy.

Diversity Must Be Institutionalized

A Natural Force such as diversity should be institutionalized. It must be more powerful than any one individual's support or resistance. When these values become part of the core values of the organization, no single person can stop this force. However, if it is not managed, the same power that is harnessed by the concept of diversity will cause enormous loss of momentum as employees focus their energies on establishing programs to address these issues. In the absence of diversity programs and initiatives, there is likely to be a great deal of resentment and frustration on the part of those who feel they are being left out because they don't fit the corporate mold in one way or another. It is impossible to even begin measuring the losses in productivity and employee contributions that may be caused by these exclusionary practices.

As the demographics of organizations become more and more diverse, this Natural Force will continue to gain momentum and be even more dominant in the future. If an organization has not already initiated a diversity program, its managers will soon realize that they have placed the company at a great disadvantage. By failing to recognize the power that exists in the Diversity Natural Force, they may themselves become victims of its adverse influence.

Managing Diversity

Diversity often challenges the "good old boy" networks that exist in many organizations. Diversity as well as affirmative action and equal opportunity laws create new opportunities for individuals who do not fit the traditional corporate or organizational mold. Diversity means more than differences in age, race, and gender. It also includes variation in such attributes as length of service, education, experience, background, and even birth order or personality style.

Diversity awareness is always important, but it becomes particularly so when organizations expand globally. New perspectives need to be encouraged in all situations, not just for a few specially designated programs earmarked for maximum visibility in this area. Today, most major organizations, big and small, are just beginning to appreciate the true power of this Natural Force. The challenge is that diversity can force you to make decisions that run contrary to your organization's traditional thinking, which can make decision makers very uncomfortable. Diversity-related decisions often involve great risks, but they also promise great paybacks and rewards.

Look Through the Diversity Lens

Organizations must constantly look through the diversity lens when making decisions and implementing policies. The power of this force will quickly be discovered as those with different viewpoints and perspectives are recognized and acknowledged. It will also be apparent when diversity is not part of the organization's decision-making processes. Diversity exists in ways that organizations may not even realize. Empowerment programs are actually based on the concept of diversity. By encouraging input and viewpoints from employees at all levels of the organization, this Natural Force creates better decisions that more accurately reflect the needs and interests of all stakeholders.

For example, in one organization, managers finally began to understand the value of this Natural Force and started soliciting opinions from different levels of the organization before they made major decisions that could potentially affect everyone. They were shocked by how differently their decisions turned out when they understood these diverse perspectives. Their decisions reflected the needs of more people, customers as well as employees. The organization learned that perpetuating the "that's the way we do things around here" attitude was often very disheartening to many whose needs were never considered in the process. They also found that decisions based on their new process led to far fewer problems and unpleasant surprises.

Create Organizational Commitment

Even if an organization generates a great deal of publicity and achieves visibility for its diversity policies, it may still harbor many obstacles to true diversity, including disagreements as to the real meaning of the word. Contrary to the organization's policy statements and fancy brochures on the subject, the behavior that is reinforced most will continue to be the norm. Forces such as diversity require support from top management in order to exist. Without it, they simply won't survive. They will get swept aside in the tide of seemingly more pressing or important priorities.

That said, there are also times when this support can be counterproductive. If support for programs such as diversity becomes a singularly driven organizational value (that is, if only one influential person is sponsoring such initiatives), they will often succeed or fail depending on a key top manager's support or lack thereof. The system works fine as long as that sponsor is still in a position of power. But what if he or she is no longer there? Will the heirapparent still sponsor initiatives such as diversity? This is the true test of an organization's commitment to such concepts and philosophies.

Synergy and Diversity

Synergy is a very powerful force that arises as a by-product of diversity. In fact, it can be achieved only through diversity. The word *synergy* describes a situation in which the whole is greater than the sum of its parts. Organizationally speaking, it means that the accomplishments of the total company are worth more than the accomplishments of its individual parts added together.

Teamwork

Synergy is what makes teamwork so effective. It is the combining of people's talents, experiences, and motivation into a shared force or energy that redefines the possibilities of working together.

The popularity of teamwork within organizations is cyclical in nature. Organizations will initially get excited about the potential of teamwork and begin to sponsor programs to promote and nurture its adoption. Unfortunately, however, this initial enthusiasm can quickly dissipate in the wake of a setback or disappointing result—which more often than not can be traced to poor implementation or mismanagement of the teamwork concept.

There are many other factors that can negatively affect the process when the idea of teamwork is introduced into an organization, including lack of management support, poor role definition within the new organizational design, turf wars, and supervisors' fears that a new team-based model will make them obsolete. This last point merits further explanation.

A key element of the teamwork concept is giving employees greater decision-making and problem-solving responsibilities in their areas of expertise. Clearly, the person doing the job knows more about how to improve his or her work than anyone else in the organization. If you are to successfully implement a teamwork initiative in an organization, you must first make sure that the supervisors of those employees who will be empowered with greater decision-making ability understand and are comfortable with what their roles will be in the new scheme of things. If they are not, they will naturally be concerned about their own job security. The question on their minds will be, "If the people I supervise are now going to make many of the decisions I have been making, what will I do?" If you can't answer this question, don't expect supervisors to embrace the concept of teamwork with any degree of enthusiasm or excitement. More likely, they will find a way to make it go away. This is likely the cause of more failed teamwork initiatives than any other single factor.

Mergers and Acquisitions

The ultimate goal of any merger or acquisition must be to achieve synergy through the diversity of the organizations being combined. If you examine any written or stated objective of such an action, you will find some reference to the concept of synergy. The companies are hoping to achieve together something that was not possible when they were on their own. They want their union to be greater than the sum of its parts. The success of the acquisition or merger depends on creating this synergy between the companies. They may achieve it in many different and creative ways, for example, by combining technologies or marketing strategies or by pooling talents. Everyone involved in the merger or acquisition will be asked to contribute to this synergy in some way.

Without synergy as a goal, the union will be far less likely to succeed, and the outcome may be that parts of the newly formed organization will be stripped away in order to reduce redundancies after the separate entities are combined. Even when synergy is the goal, organizations do not always achieve it for any number of reasons. Failure to capitalize on the potential synergy of both organizations is most likely due to poor management of the merger. Another common mistake is to underestimate the difficulty of achieving synergy in the combined organization. Synergy isn't something that just automatically happens—it must be planned for and managed. Organizations have to set the stage so that synergy will develop, and, once established, it must be nurtured so that it will grow and flourish.

The culture of the newly formed organization should be designed to include recognition and appreciation of its own augmented diversity. Investments in supporting diversity and encouraging synergy must be part of overall expenditures for the transition process. Management committees should ensure that this synergy exists to the greatest extent possible between the newly combined organizations. Upper management in particular must regularly review progress on creating and maintaining synergy. Without synergy, chances of achieving the business objectives of the acquisition or merger are greatly diminished. Too often, everyone concentrates on the technical or financial aspects of an acquisition or merger at the expense of diversity, which ultimately becomes the most important factor in achieving the business objectives of the deal.

People often make huge assumptions concerning the ease with which they can merge the diverse cultures of the two organizations. In the process, important and meaningful cultural symbols and traditions of each company's employees may be ignored or, even worse, insensitively destroyed, while management communications concerning the transition and subsequent developments will probably be nonexistent.

The term *acquisition arrogance* is used when the aggressor organization believes it will be able to manage the acquired organization better than the current leadership does. This attitude shows no respect for the diversity that the other company can bring to the combined organization. Acquisition or merger teams should have plans in place to achieve synergy between the combined organizations. If you are the target of such a takeover or purchase, you must be keenly aware of the need for diversity in this process. If the leaders of the other company don't have such a plan, help them develop one right away. Volunteer to be involved in the cultural integration process. Let them know what elements of your organization's culture are important and sacred to everyone. Join forces with the new company, for you are now part of its culture, even if you do not agree with its current ideology. Help the members of the other organization understand that one of the most valuable assets they just acquired is the diversity your company can contribute to their organization.

Embracing Diversity

A wonderful example of diversity and synergy at work can be found in the island country of Mauritius, which lies in the Indian Ocean, 1,240 miles off the southeastern coast of Africa. The story of Mauritius is the subject of a video produced by the Covey Leadership Center and is part of the training program based on Stephen Covey's (1989) book *The 7 Habits of Highly Effective People*.

There are many inherent reasons why Mauritius should fail as a country. It lacks natural resources, is isolated from the rest of the world, and consists of a number of distinctly different cultures all trying to live together on a tiny island of 720 square miles. Mauritius was first discovered by Dutch sailors in 1598 and was settled in 1638. Over the next several centuries, the island was inhabited by people from Africa, China, Europe, India, and Madagascar, resulting in a unique blend of races and cultures.

Mauritius succeeds as a country despite these potential disadvantages. It thrives, in fact, because its people consider their diversity their greatest strength. Instead of shunning those of other backgrounds or fighting over their differences, they embrace their diversity. In the Covey video, citizens of Mauritius speak of what they describe as the "miracle" of Mauritius, their success at sharing their tiny island in peace and harmony despite their vast cultural differences and perspectives. Mauritius, they say, is like fruit salad, with each fruit maintaining its individual taste, rather than like marmalade, in which all flavors are blended together. They describe Mauritius as a garden consisting of different varieties of flowers and say that this diversity is what makes the garden beautiful. In Mauritius, each individual's right to be different is respected. When you ask a question in Mauritius, everyone is not expected to give the same answer. This, they find, is a strength, not a vulnerability or a weakness.

Recent statistics confirm that we are increasingly becoming a more diverse society. According to data compiled from the 2000 U.S. census, we are now beginning to see significant changes in our national demographics. The eventual impact of these shifting demographics and the resulting diversity will not be known for some time. However, there is no question that the influence of this growing diversity will be felt by everyone in one way or another. We cannot even begin to imagine its influence on our organizational policies and practices.

Much of the new communications tools available today, such as the Internet and other electronic communications, provide access to information that has the potential to knock down barriers to diversity throughout the world, for the more we understand about different people and their cultures, the less different they become. Harnessing the power of this Natural Force can be one of the most important advancements of the new millennium. You have only to let your imagination wander for a moment to begin to conceive of these amazing possibilities.

Diversity, as much as any other Natural Force, will prevail with or without your permission or awareness. It can sneak up on you slowly. You may not be fully aware of the changes created by diversity, which acts in the same way that water flowing over a rock will alter the rock's shape and appearance over time. All of a sudden, you may realize that things are different, more diverse than they were before. You can't fight diversity any more than you can defeat any Natural Force. When we finally realize that everyone's opinion and perspective are important, we will begin to really appreciate the diversity of our world and its people. Indeed, the garden grows more beautiful every day.

The following chart is a quick reference for the Diversity Natural Force. It provides examples of ways in which to better manage or influence this force, specific actions or programs you might implement, and the impact these actions could have on employees.

Quick Reference for the Diversity Natural Force		
INFLUENCE ON NATURAL FORCE	MANAGEMENT ACTIONS	IMPACT ON EMPLOYEES
Diversity awareness training	Sponsor employee programs designed to create greater awareness of diversity issues.	Increases awareness of and sensitivity to diversity issues and the organization's commitment to achieving diversity in the workplace.
Affirmative action/ equal employment opportunity	Comply with laws and regulations regarding minority and female representation in various positions.	Gives minority and female employees more opportunities to be hired by or advance within the company.
Thinking unconventionally	Challenge organizational norms and customs to create greater diversity in the company.	Encourages thinking outside the box concerning diversity if given an example to emulate.
Diversity councils	Provide support and direction for diversity initiatives (most effective if chaired by a member of top management).	Shows that diversity is a major priority for the organization.
Image	Make diversity part of the organization's advertisements and/or publications.	Employees will know if the image is real or just a public relations initiative and will respond accordingly.

Growth

Mission   Communication   Change   Survival   Growth   Renewal   Equity   Performance   Discovery   Diversity

LAWS OF THE GROWTH NATURAL FORCE

- Organizations must grow if they are to survive.

- Growth doesn't necessarily mean bigger.

- Growth is a by-product of other natural forces.

- Growth has its price.

It is only natural for people to want to grow in their careers as well as in their personal lives. As individuals and consumers, we are all constantly searching for better lives, improved products and services, and more conveniences. Businesses and organizations are always striving to be more than they are today. This is simply the Natural Force of Growth doing its job. Many of the other nine forces naturally drive this force.

Organizations Must Grow If They Are to Survive

When a business is at a mature stage in its growth, it is important that all employees understand what this may mean to both their careers and their futures. This stage in a business or product cycle may not always be a healthy situation—organizations and their products or functions do get stagnant. Every living thing has a need to grow, including organizations.

Growth is strongly linked to survival, and "grow or die" scenarios can be found in business. Either you continue to grow and keep up with the competition or you are left behind. Maintaining the status quo may no longer be a viable option, particularly given the pace of change in technology today, even though this approach may have served you well in the past.

A management philosophy that shunned growth might have worked in the past because of factors unrelated to this Natural Force, but don't expect the world to stand still for long. Sooner or later, those who have been looking for the next growth opportunity will make a discovery that causes a paradigm shift of unimaginable proportions. A stagnant approach will seem even more antiquated when new ways finally arrive.

Growth Doesn't Necessarily Mean Bigger

Contrary to common perceptions on this subject, growth doesn't always mean bigger. Organizations can grow in many other ways. Adding to the head count may be the last thing an organization should do to ensure its future viability, especially during economic downturns or times of slowing market demand. It is a challenge to continue to grow as an organization under difficult business conditions.

Growth doesn't have to come exclusively through mergers or acquisitions, although either of these strategies might be the most expedient approach. Growth can also come from within the organization. Internal growth undertaken at a manageable rate may be even more important to success. Value acquisition through growth can be achieved without resorting to external sources.

Growth Is a By-Product of Other Natural Forces

Other Natural Forces, such as change, discovery, performance, and diversity, will naturally create new opportunities in the organization. Growth is a by-product of these forces. Without a nurturing environment for growth, these other forces may not come to fruition, and the organization may deploy incompatible strategies simultaneously. For example, money may be budgeted to develop discoveries but not to support the growth they create. This will have a negative effect on discovery. You must begin to look more holistically at how all ten Natural Forces interrelate in order to avoid conflicting strategic initiatives.

Growth Has Its Price

Growth can bring many new resources, opportunities, and, most of all, hope to an organization. Everyone gets excited about the company's new direction, thinking of all the opportunities growth will bring. Managers may dream of being credited with saving the company by initiating this new adventure, which will be recognized by future generations of employees and managers as the boldest and greatest move in the organization's history. Everyone wants to be the leader of the pack, to dominate the competition and be the person all the others admire and try to emulate. No one enters a new venture planning for failure, any more than two people simultaneously prepare for divorce and decide to get married. Why would you put yourself in a situation if you thought you were going to fail?

But of course things don't always turn out as hoped or planned. Excitement eventually gives way to reality. Unexpected problems and obstacles appear, like gremlins popping up everywhere. Customers may not be receptive to the new product or service, while your critics start to grumble loudly about the many problems the growth is causing. You begin to wonder where they were with all this free advice when you were still in the planning stages. But wait a minute. Did you ask them what they thought before you went ahead with your plans for growth? Perhaps you didn't do your homework after all.

Managing Growth

Like any other Natural Force, growth must be managed. It can have a potentially destructive influence on the entire organization if it is allowed to get out of control.

Logical Versus Reckless Growth

Managers must differentiate between productive growth and counterproductive growth. Growth for growth's sake is reckless growth. It can be an all-consuming endeavor that siphons off energy and resources that the organization can ill afford to lose. Reckless growth is difficult to recognize because everyone, from the boardroom to the factory floor, gets caught up in the excitement, forgetting that growth must be justified and the organization must be ready to expand.

Successful growth comes when companies understand their strengths as well as their weaknesses and make decisions that take both factors into account. They know how to repeat the successes of the past and have learned from their own previous mistakes and those of others. They make sure their plans are well researched and carefully thought out and have prepared for contingencies and setbacks. These companies develop schedules that are both achievable and competitive, with checkpoints along the way to help them assess their progress and reevaluate their plans.

Too Much Caution Versus Too Little Caution

Recent experiences can dramatically influence an organization's propensity to propel the Growth Natural Force into action. An organization that has achieved success through this force may be more likely to support it in the future. On the other hand, a negative experience can stall future growth despite the pressures this force exerts on the organization. It can be tough to get back on that horse after being thrown to the hard ground below. Product failures can make any company more cautious the next time someone says, "Hey, I've got a great idea. Why don't we ..." The response may be the classic "let's wait and see" attitude toward future growth expenditures. The flip side of the coin, of course, is that recent successes could send an organization off on a spree, as it tries to grow too quickly or without sufficient thought or strategic planning.

Analyzing Risk Versus Taking Action

Before diving headfirst into a venture, a company must fully understand the downside as well as the potential returns of the endeavor. Although failure is always a possibility, organizations often don't fully appreciate this type of analysis, even when considerable resources are at stake. A risk assessment may not guarantee success, but such a preparatory step can improve your awareness of the likelihood of success in a given situation.

The only risky aspect of analysis is that it may become a paralyzing exercise in itself. Many companies are guilty of analysis to paralysis in their decision-making processes. They spend so much time trying to decide whether they should do something that by the time they are ready to move, it is too late. Others may have already beaten them to the punch. The first one to market is often the one who reaps the rewards of risks.

Obviously there must be a balance between the two approaches. You need to assess the risks and then make a decision within a competitive time frame. Otherwise you may be allowing this Natural Force to take control of your resources. You must find the balance between swift action and proper analysis that will ensure successful growth for your organization.

A Time to Grow

Timing is also important in managing growth. Tapping into this force at a time when it can't be sustained is a frequent problem, which usually leads to very unfavorable results. The courts are filled with the bankruptcy cases of companies that tried to grow at the wrong time and in reckless ways.

The opportunity for growth can present itself unexpectedly. Growth might be the last thing on everyone's mind. At other times, it may require coaxing or active pursuit. Regardless of the situation, the concept of growth as a Natural Force must be understood by everyone in the organization.

Growing Pains

Growth seldom comes without a price—be it financial or in the form of additional responsibilities for employees. If the organization is going through a growth period, employees need to understand that all the growing pains they are experiencing will be worthwhile and meaningful in the end. They will want to know how this growth can benefit them personally in their careers.

The question "What's in it for me?" is a fair one and deserves an answer. If the answer is "nothing," then employees should know this. However, it is unlikely that this would ever truly be the case. Growth brings opportunity, and it requires astute management to create the greatest amount of opportunity for as many people in your organization as possible. The worst thing to do when dealing with this Natural Force is to give employees all the work that goes into organizational growth but none of the benefits.

Understand the Consequences of Not Growing

Conversely, if there is an absence of growth, as is sometimes the case in mature or shrinking markets and industries, people need to understand the problems they might encounter. The dynamics of an organization that is experiencing this Natural Force will not be present in a company that is not growing, which creates an unnatural situation for the organization. Much like humans, organizations need the dynamics of the Growth Natural Force in order to function in a healthy manner; they need to progress through natural growth cycles. Without growth, the organization tends to become complacent. It may avoid the risks of rapid change, but it will also miss out on the progress that accompanies growth. Ultimately, the organization's performance might be negatively affected, which could have an influence on careers and personal growth opportunities. The result will be reduced progress toward goal attainment for everyone.

Important Questions to Ask About Growth

Organizations must consider the long-term viability of growth. In other words, you must look several steps down the road. Ask yourself some of the following questions before you begin moving forward with a growth initiative. Without at least some understanding of the answers to these questions, you could be unleashing the power of this Natural Force on your organization without exercising control or providing direction.

- Where will you find the expertise to grow in your chosen direction?

- How will you get everyone in your organization on board with regard to this growth initiative?

- Do you have the financial resources and support you need to sustain this growth even during difficult times?

- What is the competition doing that could spoil your growth plans?

- How will your customers respond to growth in this direction?

- What other events could occur that might affect the success of your plans?

- What is the one thing that could happen that would kill your growth initiative most quickly?

- What will be the consequences if this growth initiative doesn't work?

- What might become obsolete in your organization as a result of this growth and how soon could this happen?

- Is the organization prepared to handle the success that comes with growth?

Success brings with it many new challenges. It will change your organization in ways that you can't imagine. For instance, you will probably need more sophisticated systems and processes of all kinds to meet the demands attached to success. You may require more resources, both physical and intellectual, and you may have to expand and bring in new talent to meet these increased demands. In short, part of your contingency planning for any growth initiative should be not only what you will do if it fails but what you will do if it succeeds.

Lessons for Growing

The following lessons are about growth in organizations. We often have to experience many of these lessons for ourselves before we fully comprehend their meaning and implications. Perhaps you have already been through and learned some of these lessons. Or perhaps you haven't yet faced the kind of situation that compels you to make difficult decisions about growth. Regardless, the following suggestions can help you manage this Natural Force as you begin to lead your organization forward.

Look at Problems as Opportunities for Growth

Growth doesn't always occur in obvious or predictable ways. It can happen as a result of experiences and circumstances that may appear to be something else, such as a problem. We usually don't appreciate the value of these opportunities when they occur, for we are too consumed by the situation itself to see any of its potential benefits. It may be that we see growth for what it really is only after the pressure is off. Realizing that a growth opportunity has occurred is an important part of benefiting from the experience. You need to sit down and think about what you can learn from the problem or mistake and how to avoid repeating it.

Understand Growth's Learning Curve

Growth is just like learning to ride a bicycle: you should expect to fall off a few times and skin your knee in the process. We often confuse our position on the learning curve with mastery of the skill or task we are trying to accomplish. You are bound to have a few setbacks and failures along the way. As mentioned above, it is important to grow from these experiences and consider them part of the learning process.

It is a good idea to develop a learning curve model when beginning any endeavor in which something new is being developed. Set timetables and benchmarks along this learning curve and measure your performance against your goals. That way, you can break down a major project into more manageable increments. It also allows you to provide recognition at each step in the process. This can be important, particularly with larger projects whose completion may take a long time. People who are working hard on the project need to know that they are on the right track and that you are still interested in what they are doing.

Study a Project but Don't Take Years to Do It

Experimentation is the basis of growth. This means you must be willing to try different things, but if you take too long studying a project, you could find yourself behind the competition. Conducting study after study as you seek to validate a growth opportunity may only be a waste of valuable resources, including time that could be better spent on implementing the initiative. This doesn't mean that you shouldn't do your homework, but it does mean that you shouldn't keep checking it over and over again to make sure it is correct. When you think you have it right, move ahead with some sense of urgency.

Be Willing to Be Surprised

We too often dismiss surprises as interruptions or diversions that distract us from overall progress. We become so focused on the task at hand that we ignore or dismiss too quickly some of the greatest opportunities that come our way. It might be a call from a customer asking for a product or service that we don't currently offer. Or something that didn't go as we expected reveals itself to be the beginning of a great discovery. Many of the most important discoveries and inventions occurred by accident and were not the intended outcome of the creator. Be willing to be pleasantly surprised. It might be the greatest growth opportunity you have ever experienced.

Follow the Lead of the Growth Natural Force

The best way to achieve results is to let things follow their natural course. Many organizations invest their efforts in trying to change the direction that is an inherent part of the energy of every force, but they manage only to slow it down for a while until it eventually regains its momentum.

Growth is best achieved in ways that naturally flow forward. If you allow this force to move in its natural direction, it will tell you where it wants to go. By supporting rather than resisting this direction, you will find growth a much easier and more economical process. For example, if there are certain natural outgrowths of your business, and it makes perfect sense to pursue them, that need will become apparent to you in any number of ways. If you pay attention to the direction indicated by these needs, you will see where this force is leading your organization.

Help Those Who Want to Grow

Statistically, about 20 percent of the employees of any organization really want to grow and perform professionally to their very highest potential. These people will typically be your top performers. Identify that 20 percent of the organization and provide enriching growth experiences for them. By doing this, you will eventually raise the performance bar for everyone. Think of what the coach of any sports team must do in order to make his or her team competitive. The coach will typically build the team around one or more star athletes, and the team's success usually depends on their performance. These stars certainly wouldn't be able to perform at this higher level without their teammates, but they are often the ones who make the difference between victory and defeat. Their excellent performance can lead everyone to higher levels. These stars typically share many common characteristics. They are often the ones who work the hardest, enjoy the game the most, and are most dedicated to improving their performance. There is a reason why they are the best. They are willing to do what it takes to grow a little better every day.

For an executive, working on a volunteer board can be a most humbling and valuable growth opportunity. The usual politics of power and leverage are different or may even be nonexistent on a volunteer board. What matters most is your personal influence, dedication, and hard work as you help the organization achieve its mission or support its cause. Your value is based more on your contribution to the organization than on your position in a profit-based enterprise. Volunteer managers don't have numerous resources, including administrative assistants to do the work for them. They need to get things done with the help of people who want to contribute because they believe in what they are doing, not because their bosses told them to do it.

The following chart is a quick reference for the Growth Natural Force. It provides examples of ways in which to better manage or influence this force, specific actions or programs you might implement, and the impact these actions could have on employees.

Quick Reference for the Growth Natural Force		
INFLUENCE ON NATURAL FORCE	MANAGEMENT ACTIONS	IMPACT ON EMPLOYEES
Expansion plans	Decide to invest in growing the business both physically and by head count.	Creates new career opportunities.
Acquisitions and mergers	Combine new businesses to form a potentially successful venture.	Necessitates adjustment to the changes growth brings.
Increased production capacity	Attempt to capitalize on opportunities to expand production by increasing capacity.	Changes status quo: Employees may move to higher-level positions or may lose their jobs due to excess production capacity.
Increased performance	Set more aggressive performance goals for the organization.	Requires working harder, smarter, or both.
Hiring	Decide to grow the organization by increasing head count.	Existing employees may have access to new opportunities or may feel as if they have been passed over.
Technological advances	Introduce new methods of achieving goals.	Can make jobs easier and more productive, or can make their services obsolete.
Market demands	Respond by trying to meet increasing demands and capitalize on opportunities.	Creates more work, more pay, and possibly new opportunities.
World economies	Respond to changes created by world economies.	Employees often feel they are on a roller-coaster ride of world economies that can change with little or no notice and that is not in their control.

Renewal

Mission   Communication   Change   Survival   Renewal   Equity   Performance   Discovery   Diversity   Growth

LAWS OF THE RENEWAL NATURAL FORCE

- Renewal has its own agenda.

- Renewal is part of evolutionary cycles.

- Renewal must be nurtured.

- Renewal often meets with resistance.

Renewal is similar to change in that it is the beginning of something different, but it is focused more on the continuation of natural cycles. Renewal constantly redefines the way we live our lives, often presenting us with new approaches to doing familiar things. It can show us places we have seen before but allows us to view them afresh, as if for the very first time. This force renews our interest and motivation to continue trying to improve our lives. Without renewal, organizations quickly become stale and outdated and eventually obsolete. Renewal creates the future. It is what makes each day an adventure, a chance to start again, a familiar cycle that is nevertheless full of surprises.

Renewal Has Its Own Agenda

Renewal may occur before it is needed or expected. People are usually at least fairly content with the status quo when they are unaware that there might be a better way. For example, no one was clamoring for the ability to access the World Wide Web before the introduction of the Internet. People were used to going to the library to do research, but they can now accomplish this task from their homes, using personal computers. Similarly, most people today don't feel that they simply can't exist without wireless access to this same technology, although in the future they may consider it an absolute necessity.

Renewal Is Part of Evolutionary Cycles

As the saying goes, everything repeats itself. Cycles are a force in themselves, enabling renewal to occur. Managers must be able to recognize and understand cycles in order to develop greater predictive abilities.

The life cycles of products and services provide an excellent example of the Renewal Natural Force. Products and services have natural life cycles of their own. Without renewal, they become obsolete through lack of development. By the time you begin to realize this inevitable fact, your competition is often already on to the next generation of product or service. Those who don't understand the Natural Force of Renewal will not appreciate that it is part of an evolutionary process. Renewal is really about evolution.

Renewal Must Be Nurtured

Unfortunately, there are no sirens going off at the end of cycles to alert us that the natural life of a product or service is drawing to a close. In fact, this part of the cycle might be the most profitable period of its entire lifetime. The product or service has become a cash cow in the minds of managers, and they want to extract as much money from it as possible. Cash cows are often milked dry for this reason and are incapable of ever producing again.

Renewal is like planting a seed from a mature tree and tilling the soil to help it grow. There are many renewing forces constantly at play in an organization, but resources must be updated once in a while so that renewal can proceed. Old factories have to be modernized, policies should be revisited, and structures require redesign. Without nurturing, the resource will be incapable of perpetuating itself and will eventually fade away.

The Renewal Natural Force is always at work on virtually every aspect of the organization, for no sooner is something begun than it starts to become outdated. This Natural Force often needs more care and attention than the others do. You have to create the conditions that allow renewal to flourish.

Renewal Often Meets with Resistance

Renewing a successful resource may interfere with its productivity. For this reason, proposals that affect a currently successful product or service, even if intended to ensure its continued success, are often met with resistance—particularly if they might interrupt the positive cash flow produced by the resource.

The Natural Force of Renewal faces many challenges in an organization. It is similar to the Natural Force of Change in that people will find many reasons to resist it in their organizations. Money, capital, budgets, and careers invested in current systems are all obstacles to renewal. Conservation of the organization's resources is often a very compelling argument and is hardest to counter during tough economic times. Foresight and vision are needed to support renewal in the face of these obstacles. Without renewal, the organization will eventually cease to exist. An organization's health depends on well-managed evolutionary change.

The Evolutionary Cycle Model

The evolutionary cycle model shown in Figure 2 can apply to a number of organizational processes, such as products, services, or even management philosophies and practices. This model represents the evolutionary cycle that exists when the renewal process is permitted to follow its natural course. In terms of this cycle, evolution may take a long time, or, as in the case of the dot-com companies, it can occur at a considerably faster pace. Without an understanding of the position of a product, service, or process in the evolutionary cycle, you may be fighting the Natural Force of Renewal, and this will ultimately prove to be a losing battle.

Conception

The evolutionary cycle begins with the conception of a new idea. This is obviously the most important step in the entire process. If more time and thought were invested at this stage, there would be fewer failed attempts at growth. A bad idea, no matter how well executed, is still a bad idea.

Development

Development is always necessary to turn ideas into realities. Some people are much better at conception than at development, and the reverse is true as well. In these two stages, different types of people can complement one another's strengths and weaknesses.

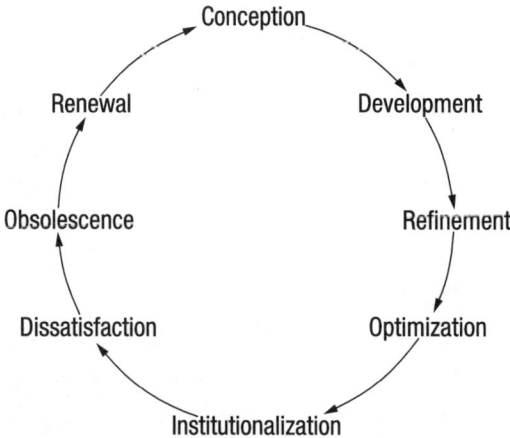

Figure 2   The Evolutionary Cycle

Too often, an idea looks great on paper but can't be scaled up into a practical, producible product. There can be innumerable obstacles in the way of bringing the idea to fruition. Overcoming these obstacles is a management skill requiring knowledge of the organization's systems, processes, personnel, politics, resources, and so on, and a mastery of how to use these various elements to move a project forward. When acquired, this skill can be a significant force in any organization.

Refinement

During the refinement stage, you begin to get the bugs out of your idea. Sometimes, a product or system never really progresses beyond this point. You may not be able to get the concept to work, at least not in the way it was originally envisioned. Sometimes the cycle stops here, to be continued at a later date. Perhaps all the necessary elements are not yet available, or the timing is not right.

Optimization

When something is optimized, it is "as good as it gets." No matter what is done to try to improve it, it probably will not change appreciably. Optimization might also be called *peak performance*. If the cycle reaches this stage, things are probably going as well as they possibly can. Most or all of the problems have been worked out, and you are making good progress. By this stage, the new product or system is gaining greater acceptance and perhaps popularity, which leads to the next step.

Institutionalization

When something becomes institutionalized, it becomes part of the organization. Becoming part of the organization has both a positive and a negative side. On the plus side, the new product or system has become the new way of doing things, the norm. On the downside, once something becomes institutionalized, it can be more difficult to change or even eliminate.

Dissatisfaction

Sooner or later, people become disenchanted with current methods and technologies. They begin searching once again for the proverbial better mousetrap. The new system or product may begin to display certain inadequacies, causing it to fall just short of expectations. As time goes by, these shortfalls become bigger and more apparent. The cycle continues until it reaches the point at which the once latest and greatest appears outdated and obsolete, which leads to the next phase in the cycle.

Obsolescence

Like extinction, which is also part of the natural process of evolution, obsolescence is inevitable. Everything becomes obsolete at some point. Obsolescence isn't necessarily bad; it is a natural part of the renewal process. Obsolescence is actually desirable sometimes, because it makes way for the new and begins the renewal cycle. Without obsolescence, the world would change much more slowly. Obsolescence is accelerated by other Natural Forces, such as the Natural Force of Discovery.

Obsolescence is sometimes designed into a product so that consumers will replace parts or buy new products on a predictable schedule. This strategy works until a competitor introduces a product with a longer life cycle and the consumer realizes the difference. The American automobile industry found itself in this situation in the 1980s, when its strategy of planned obsolescence compelled customers to buy new cars every three years or so. The strategy worked fine until the Japanese introduced cars that were built to a higher standard and began making considerable inroads into the American automobile market.

Obsolescence should not be confused with renewal. Otherwise, suggestions for or attempts at renewal will often be greeted with great resistance. Obsolescence is a state in which we should be getting rid of something because it no longer works and replacing it with something that does. Obsolescence is the step before renewal— it doesn't end the cycle.

Renewal

Renewal is the process of starting over. It is the force that continues the evolutionary cycle. Renewal usually comes at the end of the cycle, but the cycle may be interrupted at any of the evolutionary stages. A paradigm-shifting event or circumstance may occur and send you back to the beginning at any time, with the Renewal Natural Force moving to center stage. Organizations that embrace the concept of renewal are most successful at sustaining their initial gains. Their goal is to strive constantly to achieve higher levels of quality and customer satisfaction.

Managing Renewal

Renewal often happens only through the intervention of management. Success doesn't last forever, and there may be forces at work that cause success to be short-lived unless there is intervention.

Interventions may take the form of decisions such as, for example, initiating the redesign of a popular automobile even though sales of the current model are still strong. Consumers may wonder why auto companies are constantly changing the designs of their cars. The answer is simple—companies want to renew the public's interest in a familiar model. Politicians, too, understand this renewal principle and are perpetually trying to reinvent themselves.

The computer industry is another business that operates in a constant state of renewal. As soon as you leave the store with the most cutting-edge computing technology, an upgraded version of the product is released. For example, Microsoft realized that its future depended on creating even better products. The company launched a huge research and development effort in 2001, spending in excess of $4 billion. This was more than the combined research expenditures of all its major competitors. Microsoft's plan was to build on its very profitable franchises for desktop and server software by moving into markets that were new to the company, such as game consoles, small business software, and Web services. The organization continued to look ahead, with contingency plans that ensured its continued success regardless of possible events outside its direct influence and control. This is the Renewal Natural Force at work, fulfilling its mission.

Efficiency is doing things right; effectiveness is doing the right things. There is a big difference. Just because you are doing things right doesn't mean you are doing the right things. You might be preserving processes or products that need to progress to their natural end points. You don't want to invest your energies in becoming expert or even proficient at something that is outdated and ineffective. Allowing natural evolution to develop without a compatible vision creates systems that are self-defeating, redundant, and obsolete. Many companies found themselves in this position in the past decades and consequently no longer exist.

Honoring the Past

Renewal is an effective management strategy because it retains at least some of the benefits of the past. The more opportunities you provide for renewal, the more natural energy will be rediscovered in your organization.

Inertia can also be a powerful force for those who have spent time in a stagnant work environment, and it may have to be phased out in stages. As renewal is introduced, employees should participate through a planned process that allows sequential transition and honors past traditions. Change is more palatable when it is introduced in ways that respect the past. Simply by recognizing the contributions of the past, you may find that renewal is accepted more readily by everyone involved. In addition, people often need time to move from the old to the new. Give them a chance to get their bearings and concentrate on where they are headed in the future. A small investment in helping employees deal with the changes that result from renewal will yield significant returns in terms of acceptance and cooperation.

We need to learn from the past and continue to grow and improve each day. Renewal starts everything over again. This Natural Force sometimes offers us a second chance to get things right. If we don't grow each day, we have lost the opportunity to become better tomorrow. Failure is not the worst thing that can happen. It is much worse not to learn from our mistakes, for this means we will be repeating them into the future.

Envisioning the Future

In the smoldering wreckage of the dot-com industry lie a few brave souls who are still willing to believe that technology will one day regain its former position of prominence on the business scene. Not surprisingly, one of these leaders was General Electric's former legendary chairman, John F. Welch. While others were lying low during the collapse of the high-technology industry, Welch was leading his company back into the battle for market share, working toward fulfilling his vision of "digitizing" every aspect of the company. In 2001, the company's plans included spending $3 billion on high tech, up 12 percent and three times the industry average during that period. Many companies are ignoring this Natural Force and are failing to renew their resources and commitment in the high-tech arenas. They will be the ones left behind when the industry does reinvent and resurrect itself. It takes vision to see the signs of renewal all around, especially when the view is blocked by today's problems and agendas.

Reinventing Yourself

The business environment is constantly in a state of flux, and each new day brings new challenges to face. Perhaps the most important lesson for any organization to learn is how to master the Natural Force of Renewal. Organizations need to continuously reinvent themselves, redefining their missions and adapting to the business environment in which they compete. In the marketplace jungle, it can be a matter of survival of the fittest, and those who are most adaptable are most likely to survive.

It is not easy for companies to keep reinventing themselves. Like change, moving into businesses and ventures outside your core competencies can be both scary and dangerous. But taking bold moves is an absolute necessity, particularly in the age of technology, with its rapid pace of change. Early computer technology leader Wang avoided introducing new products for fear they would destroy the market for its existing ones. This once successful company didn't appreciate the necessity of renewing itself and was replaced by others offering updated versions of Wang's own products. Organizations ultimately have to take some risks—there is no sure bet when it comes to success.

Organizations need renewal strategies that take into account as many factors as possible that might exert some influence on the future. They must constantly evaluate their products and services to determine if their current offerings are continuing to serve them well. And most important, they must create a culture that supports the concept of renewal and sponsors its existence on a daily basis.

By its very definition, the renewal process is never ending; however, in order to capitalize on the power of this Natural Force, you must nurture it faithfully and consistently. Sometimes you just have to let go of something that served you well in the past but shows signs of becoming the proverbial albatross around your neck. Companies that insist on conservatism at all costs constantly make the mistake of holding on to a product or a market when such actions can no longer be justified and may be damaging to organizational health.

If there is any one Natural Force that can have the most significant influence on your life, it is renewal. Incorporate this Natural Force into your short-term and longer-range strategic planning, and you will find yourself continuously finding new and better ways in which to live and prosper every day.

The following chart is a quick reference for the Renewal Natural Force. It provides examples of ways in which to better manage or influence this force, specific actions or programs you might implement, and the impact these actions could have on employees.

Quick Reference for the Renewal Natural Force

INFLUENCE ON NATURAL FORCE	MANAGEMENT ACTIONS	IMPACT ON EMPLOYEES
Long-range strategic planning	Create a plan that may become reality in the future.	Knowing the plan enables them to support it and help make it a reality.
Reorganizations	Create a new version of the organization, hoping the result will be an improvement over the original.	Necessitates adaptation to the new structure.
Restructuring	Redesign organizational systems with the aim of improving their efficiency.	If they understand management objectives, they will try to adjust to new systems.
Goal setting	Establish new goals, hoping to renew its successes.	Employees work toward achieving goals with greater commitment if they feel some ownership of the objectives.
Mergers/ takeovers	Aggressor company tries to create a new organization that incorporates the best of the acquired organization.	Creates uncertainty about their roles in the new organization if not made clear to them.
Acquisitions	Acquiring company attempts to create synergy between the two or more organizations being combined.	Causes concern about their roles in the newly created organization.
Divestitures	Attempt to limit losses by divesting those sections that are no longer meeting expectations.	May result in lost jobs or displacement to other jobs.

Planning for the Natural Forces

You cannot change the weather; you may not even be able to predict it. But you can learn to plan for it. For example, planning ahead helps you avoid the many inconveniences and problems rain might cause you. You could also capitalize on the situation by planting flowers in anticipation of the rain. Similarly, learning to plan for the ten Natural Forces will help you use their energy to your benefit and give you an advantage over your competition.

The Natural Forces will be an influential factor for you and your organization as long as you are in business. They are more powerful than anyone in your organization. They will dominate every business day, in one way or another. As a leader in your organization, you should strive to gain a better understanding of these Natural Forces and their influence and power, and you must also plan with their influence in mind and adjust your business strategy accordingly. Otherwise, you might find yourself trying to survive in today's competitive business environment without shelter from the storm.

Working in Harmony with the Natural Forces

When you achieve a state of harmony, everything flows in its most natural manner. Instead of resisting Natural Forces and experiencing their negative effects, employees are moving in the same direction. This helps them feel a stronger connection with the organization. There is less wasted energy and tension. Systems and processes function more smoothly, as they were designed to do. You won't be fighting invisible forces that seem to steal away all your resources and energies, leaving you little or nothing to show in return. Harmony with the Natural Forces creates an environment that generates excitement and commitment to goals.

Creating a Natural Forces Task Force

Understanding how to incorporate awareness of the Natural Forces into your management planning and business strategy is a necessary first step. For this purpose, the Natural Forces task force is an invaluable tool. The mission of the task force should be to identify and try to understand the situations within the organization that are being affected by these Natural Forces. The task force should be charged with the responsibility of directing the Natural Forces so that the organization can achieve its goals. This is no small task, and to be done correctly, it requires the involvement of the most talented people in the organization. If their mission is successful, this task force will be one of the most positive influences on the entire organization.

A Natural Forces task force might be an ongoing entity that meets regularly, or it could be formed on an ad hoc basis. Regardless, its task should be the same—to keep these Natural Forces in the forefront of the organization's planning process. It should concentrate on examining how these Natural Forces might influence day-to-day operations as well as major projects. On the most basic level, this task force will ensure that the Natural Forces are anticipated and taken into consideration by the organization. On a more advanced level, the task force could attempt to manage these Natural Forces. And on the highest level, it could address the task of maximizing the forces to the organization's greatest advantage.

Program for the Natural Forces Task Force

The task force should take the following steps as it begins harnessing the power of these Natural Forces to help the organization reach its goals.

Educate the Organization

The task force must begin by educating the organization about these ten powerful and influential Natural Forces. This can be done in any number of ways, using this book as a starting point. The task force should seek out and communicate specific examples of the Natural Forces at work in the organization, so that all employees will understand that the Natural Forces play a part in virtually everything that happens.

Keep the Lines of Communication Open

Communication, which is a Natural Force itself, is of the greatest importance in managing the other forces. The task force must ensure that the lines of communication are always open concerning the influence of the Natural Forces. Creating this greater awareness should be one of the task force's major goals. Approaches to this objective include postings, letters, signs, newsletters, e-mails, presentations, or other internal media efforts designed to increase awareness within the entire organization.

Incorporate Natural Forces into Planning and Development

Natural Forces are already part of the way you do business. They are there regardless of whether or not you want them, so you might as well incorporate them into your planning and development. The potential influence of these Natural Forces should be part of every strategic plan and every decision. It is important to determine those factors that are under your direct control and those forces that are not. A little forewarning and preparation go a long way toward managing these Natural Forces, in much the same way that weather forecasts help you prepare for the next day's rain. You may not be able to control these Natural Forces, but you can influence your manner of reacting to them.

Develop a Long-Term Perspective

You must act with a long-term perspective when it comes to Natural Forces. Natural Forces are not a passing fad; they have always existed, and they always will. The task force should be thinking of ways to incorporate them into the organization's planning and development, not only in the immediate future, but in the long run as well. Task force members need to think ahead and try to envision how the future might be affected by these Natural Forces and begin planning for these eventualities.

Standing committees represent an effective approach to managing the Natural Forces. Create a committee composed of subgroups that are in charge of one or more of these Natural Forces. The smaller groups could meet regularly, with action-oriented agendas designed to promote their particular Natural Force or Forces. Each subgroup could use the appropriate chapters and Natural Force laws from this book as an outline as its members focus on the Natural Forces they have been assigned. The entire committee should then meet on a predetermined schedule, such as monthly or quarterly, to hear reports on the subgroups' progress and support one another's efforts.

Tapping Into the Forces' Natural Energy

Harnessing this energy to move your organization in the direction of your goals will always be the challenge. When you begin to move in conjunction with this natural energy, your goals become so much more attainable. You may be able to tap into only a minuscule fraction of the total energy these forces can provide, but even this amount will have a significant positive influence on the organization. Think of what it will be like to harness this energy to help you move in your chosen direction instead of experiencing its destructive aspects when you attempt to oppose it.

Best of all, this tremendously powerful energy source is available for free. Many of the initiatives suggested in this book require little or no additional expenditures and, in fact, could save significant amounts of money in the long run. Adopting some of these approaches may also save you much frustration and many problems in the future. Indeed, you may never be able to channel all the potential energy of these Natural Forces to your advantage, but just being able to minimize the downside can be valuable in itself.

When you do begin moving in harmony with the Natural Forces, you may feel as if you have captured lightning in a bottle. You have tapped into an energy that is of nature itself. Don't worry if you don't always understand these forces. They are among the mysteries of the universe. All you have to do is recognize and respect their power.

References

Barker, J. A. *Future Edge*. New York: Morrow, 1992.

Barker, J. A. *The New Business of Paradigms*. St. Paul, MN: Star Thrower Distribution, 2001a. Video.

Barker, J. A. *The 21ˢᵗ Century Edition*. St. Paul, MN: Star Thrower Distribution, 2001b. Video.

Barker, J. A. *Wealth, Innovation & Diversity: Putting Our Differences to Work in the 21ˢᵗ Century*. St. Paul, MN: Star Thrower Distribution, 2001c. Video.

Covey, S. *The 7 Habits of Highly Effective People*. New York: Simon & Schuster, 1989.

Jones, D. *Everyday Creativity*. St. Paul, MN: Star Thrower Distribution, 1999. Video

Senge, P. *The Fifth Discipline*. New York: Doubleday, 1990.

Suggested Reading

Chapter 1

Arndt, M., Carney, D., and Zellner, W. "The Ever-Shrinking Skies." *BusinessWeek*, January 22, 2001.

Bittel, L. L. *What Every Supervisor Should Know*. New York: McGraw-Hill, 1980.

Brick, M. "16,000 to Get Ax at Lucent." *New York Times*, January 25, 2001.

Crosby, P. B. *Quality Is Free*. New York: McGraw-Hill, 1979.

Hyde, J. "Chrysler Tries to Avoid 'Strike Three.'" *Pittsburgh Post-Gazette*, January 30, 2001.

Kahn, J. "Air Startups Hit Unexpected Turbulence." *Fortune*, January 22, 2001.

McGinn, D., and Naughton, K. "How Safe Is Your Job?" *Newsweek*, February 5, 2001.

Owen, B. "CBS Bets 'Survivor' Can Survive Bad Timing." *Pittsburgh Post-Gazette*, January 28, 2001.

Chapter 2

Barker, J. A. *Paradigms: The Business of Discovering the Future*. New York: Harper Business, 1993.

Garwood, D., and Bane, M. "Shifting Paradigms' Atlanta, GA: Dogwood Publishing, 1990.

Kessler, M. "Future Bleak for Small PC Makers." *USA Today*, January 22, 2001.

Reich, R. B. "How to Be a Change Insurgent." *Fast Company*, October 2000.

Chapter 3

Caulfield, B. "Talk Is Cheap. And Good for Sales Too." www.ecompany.com, April 2001.

Hamilton, J. "The New Sign Language." *BusinessWeek* e.biz, March 19, 2001.

Kiger, P. J. "Frequent Employee Feedback Is Worth the Cost and Time." *Workforce*, March 2001.

Patton, C. "The Grapevine." *Human Resource Executive*, January 2001.

Shevat, A. "Practicing OD with a Technology Driven Global Organization." *OD Practitioner*, 33(1), 2001.

Zeldin, T. "Talk Is Cheap. Let's Have a Conversation." *Fast Company*, December 2000.

Chapter 4

Blodgett, M. "Game Plans." *CIO Magazine*, January 15, 1998.

Cabana, P. "The Dog and Pony Show Must Go On!" *Fast Company*, February 2001.

Carroll, J. "Darth Vulture, Corporate Raider," Business2.com, December 12, 2000.

Clark, R. D., "Can You See Clearly?" *Black Enterprise,* October 2000.

Kleiner, A., Roth, G., and Kruschwitz, R. "Should a Company Have a Noble Purpose?" *Across the Board,* January 2001.

Peters, T. "Leadership Is Confusing As Hell." *Fast Company*, March 2001.

"Tied to Work." *Human Resource Executive,* January 2001.

Chapter 5

"Behind Microsoft's Comeuppance." *BusinessWeek,* January 29, 2001.

Boselovic, L. "How Fortunate!" *Pittsburgh Post-Gazette,* April 29, 2001.

Boselovic, L. "Steel Standing." *Pittsburgh Post-Gazette,* February 25, 2001.

Economides, N. "The Real Losers in the Microsoft Anti-Trust Case," *SternBusiness,* Spring/Summer 2000.

Hattiangadi, A. U., and Habib, A. M. *A Closer Look at Comparable Worth.* (2nd. ed.). Washington, DC: Employment Policy Foundation, 2000.

Kruger, P. "Why Aren't There More Women at the Top?" *Fast Company,* August 2000.

Lavelle, L. "Executive Pay" *BusinessWeek,* April 16, 2001.

McKay, J. "LTV, USW Heads to Meet as Talks Founder." *Pittsburgh Post-Gazette,* April 29, 2001.

Samuelson, R. "Indifferent to Inequality?" *Newsweek,* May 7, 2001.

Chapter 6

Balu, R. "Bonuses Aren't Just for the Bosses." *Fast Company,* December 2000.

Balu, R. "Mike Espy Is No Stranger to Success." *Fast Company,* April 2001.

Barton, Z. "If the Phone Rings, Answer It." *Fast Company,* December 2000.

Clifford L. "Why You Can Safely Ignore Six Sigma." *Fortune,* January 22, 2001.

Greene, J. "A Break in the Weather for Microsoft? Not for Long." *BusinessWeek,* January 22, 2001.

Hof, R. D. "Remember the Tortoise." *BusinessWeek* e.biz, January 22, 2001.

McCormack, M. H., "What's Your Score?" *Across the Board,* March/April 2001.

Mehta, S. N., "Lessons from the Lucent Debacle." *Fortune,* February 5, 2001.

Nutt, P. C. "Half of the Decisions We Make Are Wrong. Why?" *Across the Board,* March/April 2001.

Serwer, A. "Don't Bury Tech Yet—It's Still Alive." *Fortune,* January 22, 2001.

Sutel, S. "Now Comes the Hard Part—AOL Time Warner Merger Party Dampened by Marketplace Realities." *Pittsburgh Post-Gazette,* January 13, 2001.

Varma, A., Beatty, R. W., Schneiger, C. E., and Ulrich, D. O. "High Performance Work Systems: Exciting Discovery or Passing Fad?" *Human Resource Planning,* 22(1), 1999.

Warner, M. "Pity the Poor Dot-Commer (a Little Bit)." *Fortune,* January 22, 2001.

Weber, J., Anderson-Forest, S., Symonds, W. C., and Byrnes, N. "The BusinessWeek 50." *BusinessWeek,* Spring 2001.

Chapter 7

Ante, S. E, Borrus, A., and Hof, R. D. "In Search of the Net's Next Big Thing." *BusinessWeek,* March 26, 2001.

Brown, T. "The Empowerment Myth." *Across the Board,* March/April 2001.

Cortese, A. "Masters of Innovation." The BusinessWeek 50, *BusinessWeek,* Spring 2001.

Dahle, C. "Have You Seen the Five Faces of Genius?" *Fast Company,* October 2000.

Greengard, S. "10 HR Technology Trends for 2001." *Workforce* www.workforce.com, January 2001.

Hamel, G. "Edison's Curse." *Fortune,* March 5, 2001.

Hof, R. D. "On Beyond the Web." *BusinessWeek* e.biz, March 19, 2001.

Isaacs, N. "Crash & Burn: Dot-Bomb Survivors Piece Through the Wreckage." www.upsidetoday.com, March 2001.

Malone, M. "The Amazing, Incredible SHRINKING FUTURE!" *Forbes ASAP,* April 2, 2001.

Mandel, M. J., and Hof, R. D. "Rethinking the Internet." *BusinessWeek,* March 26, 2001.

Schonfeld, E. "A Bright Idea for GE." www.ecompany.com, March 2001.

Thomke, S. "Enlightened Experimentation: The New Imperative for Innovation." *Harvard Business Review,* February 2001.

Ulfelder, S. "The Dirty Half-Dozen." www.Darwinmag.com, June 2001.

Chapter 9

Armstrong, D. "A Stick in the Spokes." *Forbes,* March 5, 2001.

Nicholson, N. "The Big Gamble." *Across the Board,* January 2001.

Schlender, B. "10 Tech Trends to Bet On." *Fortune,* March 19, 2001.

Sloan, A. "The Downside of Momentum." *Newsweek,* March 19, 2001.

Whalen, C. J., "Consumer Confidence Is No Crystal Ball." *BusinessWeek,* March 19, 2001.

Chapter 10

Charan, R., and Colvin, G. "13 Moves to Make Before Your Competitors Do Plus 3 Rules Not to Forget." *Fortune,* February 5, 2001.

Cohen, H. "The Price Is Wrong." *Industry Standard,* January 1–8, 2001.

Cole, C. L. "The Evolving, Creative American Office." *Workforce* www.workforce.com, February 2001.

Dowd, M. "Jumping the Shark." *Pittsburgh Post-Gazette,* June 7, 2001.

Drucker, P., and Senge, P. "Meeting of the Minds." *Across the Board,* November/December 2000.

Ellis, J. "It's Over and It's Just Begun." *Fast Company,* June 2001.

Garten, J. E. "The Mind of the C.E.O." *BusinessWeek,* February 5, 2001.

Greene, J. "Microsoft: How It Became Stronger Than Ever." *BusinessWeek,* June 4, 2001.

Lyons, D. "Lion in Winter." *Forbes,* April 30, 2001.

Master, M. "Overreaching." *Across the Board,* March/April 2001.

McGrath, P. "The Cost of Survival." *Newsweek,* May 14, 2001.

Rubin, H. "Roger Cass, The Last Optimist." *Fast Company,* July 2001.

Sloan, A. "Breaking Up Is (Still) Hard to Do." *Newsweek,* June 4, 2001.

Stewart, T. A. "Listen Up, Maggots! You Will Deploy a More Humane and Effective Managerial Style!" www.ecompany.com, July 2001.

Index